On An Angel's Wing

by

Marilyn Lawrence

Editorial service: Kay Derochie
Design: Fuseology Creative

Library of Congress Cataloging-in-Publication Data

Lawrence, Marilyn
On An Angel's Wing : Real-Life Angelic Encounters and Divine Lessons / Marilyn Lawrence.
   p. cm.

ISBN: 978-0-9915707-5-1

1. Angels   2. Masters   I. Title

Printed in the United States of America
Dragonfly Media, LLC

Acknowledgements

Thank you to all the beautiful souls who volunteered their heart-felt Angel stories included within these pages to create heightened awareness globally.

Thank you to Kay Derochie for her dedication and expertise in editing "our" work.
Thank you to Mary Frantz for the loving preliminary review of "our" work.
Thank you to Elizabeth McIsaac for the quote, "movies in my eyes."

Thank you to my husband, Dale, for his love and unwavering support.
Thank you to my son, Michael, for being the instrumental evaluator.

And, every morning and every evening, I send the following gratitude:

Thank you, God, Angels, ArchAngels, Ascended Masters, Masters of Wisdom, My Guides, My Council and My Guardian Angels, Fairies, Earth, Nature and Aquatic Realms, Mother Earth and Father Sky for everything you do for me, my family, my loved ones, the world, and the universe every day and every way.

Table of Contents

Preface

Welcome to the World of the Angelic Realm

Have you ever wondered whether particular experiences you encountered included Angel assistance? Are you curious about life in the Angelic realm? Have you ever wondered how an Angel becomes an Angel or wondered what happens when you pass from this life? *On An Angel's Wing* answers these questions and more.

The book is comprised of five elements: A new soul joining the Angelic realm as an "Angel-in-training" and the questions involved in her realization of such, scenes from the human life she left behind, the Angels' and Masters' training lessons and answers, real-life stories of Angel interventions, and descriptions of what the assisting Angel experiences during such real-life events.

The lessons and answers of Angels and Masters and the new Angel's questions and comments that I have recounted in this book were given to me as a gift from other realms and are recorded as delivered to me. The messages are unchanged, though I expressed some of the Angels' and Masters' lessons in the voice of the trainee to ease in comprehension. The lessons include Earth Angel qualities, how Angels provide assistance, transitions the earth and humans will be encountering, how to prepare for the transitions, and more.

Fictional elements include Violet's earth story, added so that humans can identify with the new Angel, and Gabrielle's story, added as a teaching story to accompany an Angel lesson.

After receiving the real-life Angel stories from family, friends, and their acquaintances that are included in the book, I began to wonder about the assisting Angel's side of such experiences. When I opened myself up to the Angels' involvement, I was taken to a place where I felt a part of each experience. What I wrote was from that place of guided involvement and, therefore, I trust in the truth of what I have written.

I am humbled by the Divine communications that were written through me about life in the Angelic realm. These channeled messages and the real-life Angelic encounters are shared with the full intention of raising the level of consciousness to a higher awareness in the human realm and of spreading the truth that there is help, no matter what the situation. It is important to recognize the times that have or will have the Divine touch of an Angel's Wing in support and assistance.

One simply has to ask and then pay attention, with full faith and no doubt, to the aid and encouragement received.

Enjoy!

Chapter One

Lesson of the Awakening

Still coughing and gasping for air, She slowly lifted her head keeping her eyes tightly clinched.

Gradually She was gaining consciousness, still fighting to get her breath and panicked that She could not breathe deeply without choking, She took small breaths. Fearing that the air would burn again, She automatically coughed after the inhales. Again breathing in, this time filling her lungs, She realized that the air was no longer toxic. The heavy grey air was gone, replaced by lighter air. She could now open her eyes without severe burning. Where was She? She struggled to remember. Where had She been? What had happened? Try as She might, the memories evaded her. She was unable to piece together the turn of events, pull forward the memories. Now cherishing each breath, pulling the air into her mouth, deep into her lungs, one thing She knew for sure, the air felt good. To breathe again felt good. She saw that she was enveloped in a white fog. She could not make out anything. Think, think, She told herself. She lowered her head and shook it, perhaps in an attempt to jar loose memories. "What happened? Where was I before? Where am I now? Why can't I remember anything?"

She again raised her head and began looking around. This time She was able to see some of her surroundings. Everything was white, as though She were still encircled by the fog or perhaps smoke. That's it. I was in smoke. . .but not this smoke. . .dark, hot smoke. . .I was in a fire. Where was I? Did someone rescue me; pull me from the fire, from the noxious air? Why am I alone? Where is everyone? She tried calling out, but no words came from her mouth. She could not speak. She tried again to yell. Nothing. The billowing white air swirled around her like clouds moving quickly in a brisk wind. There was no grey, dark smoke; the heaviness and darkness were gone. There was light, twinkling, sparkling light all around her. She was light.

She looked for her hands but saw none. She could no longer find a human shape to her being, She only saw a mass of sparkling, white light, radiating, almost pulsating light. She was glowing light. At the same time She felt complete happiness, complete peace, complete calm and acceptance, and a complete sense of belonging. She could *feel* and everything She felt was good.

Slowly the white foggy air began to dissipate. She looked beyond her own glowing image and saw other masses of radiating, shimmering matter moving toward her. Now all around her, She could see and feel.

Gradually a large persona unveiled itself from the haze. It appeared atop a small hill directly in front of her. As the fog dissipated, the impression became unblemished, purer. What was She looking at? What was this place? Clad in white, flowing material, the image seemed almost transparent. She felt a sense of immense joy seeing it and had a sense of complete acceptance emanating from this impression. Like sparkling diamonds converging, the impression gained more solidity coalescing into a figure that moved slightly. She noticed, protruding from the figure's shoulders, large beautiful wings, so significant they touched the ground.

She felt humble in front of this figure. She felt as though She were graced. She automatically lowered her head in a sign of respect. Other glowing masses began to form and become more distinct. Apparently floating, they encircled her.

Who were these beautiful beings?

What was She witnessing?

What had happened?

She looked up and listened.

Words came to her from the being with the magnificent wings. Though the figure's mouth did not move, she began to receive answers to her questions.

"You are the You that you are.

They are the They that They Are.

They are, You are, I Am.

Do not *think* any more about it.

Feel and you will know

They Are.

Feel who They Are.

You have to *Feel* to have the Vision to Know.

When you begin to feel, then you will know them much more than a name. You will know who they really are, the very essence of them."

Again She tried to speak, confused by what She had just heard, but for a second time no words came out. She projected her thoughts to the image that was communicating with her. "I cannot feel them. I cannot see anyone. I just see shimmering light masses. Who are you speaking of?"

"You cannot See until you Feel.
You cannot Feel until you Believe.
You cannot Believe until you have full Faith.
Full Faith that You Are and They Are and I Am.
Let everything else go and know now that
They Are.

Catching herself before attempting to speak, She projected her thoughts, "Where did you go? I cannot see you, I am alone again."

"You are never alone because I Am and You Are, always and One.

"I Am of You
You Are of Me
And
Together We Are
And
They Are

because I Am

and

because I Am

so too They Are, I Am."

The light and warmth of the truth of this message infused every molecule of her being. It felt true. She closed her eyes and let it in. The fidelity of the transmission impregnated her. She felt as though She had bubbles permeating her, effervescing throughout her, filling her with an illuminated light, through every cell, every micro-cell. From head to toe She felt percolated. From the very core of her inside to her outer layers She felt saturated, tingles and bubbles awakening more of her than She had ever remembered knowing. She could feel everything and She could sense more than She could ever recognize before.

All around her she could feel, They Are. She was not alone. She was warmed and surrounded. They Are and I Am.

"I feel so good, so unconditionally loved. I feel oneness with everyone and everything. I am so happy. I know that I am with you now and I do not know where I was before, but with you is where I want to stay. I want this feeling forever. Is this how you feel always?"

"We feel complete acceptance and warmth of affection constantly. We never experience the extreme sadness and lows, depression, and loneliness as some in the human realm do. On that same note, there are other feelings that we will not experience again, some of the wonderful feelings they can feel: the spike in feelings such as excitement, romance, passion. Those extremes we do not feel. We are balanced and therefore do not wave back and forth, up and down in what appears to be an uncontrollable pattern of emotions, as some humans do. Because of a lack of vision to see the greatness they are, many in the human realm do not command but let emotional dramas manipulate and influence them, reeling in a circle of sensations that could easily be controlled. There is much we are charged to do in helping other realms, but now we will focus on the human realm. Though we do not experience the roller coaster of emotions that uncontained operating creates, we do know how emotions feel. Because of our heightened senses and because many of us have lived these feelings in past lives, we simply need to recall the feelings, tastes, smells, and then these senses are a part of us. We now can feel those emotional states by recall, but we are no longer driven by them.

"Because we are pure love, we feel the constant warmth of pure love throughout, love and compassion for the greatness that each human embodies, for the pure soul that lies within each of them. We do not get angry or disgruntled when a person does something that is not in line with their pure greatness because we know that they will eventually move back onto their path again. We pray for the good in them to be strong and for the purpose they chose for this life they are living to be followed and achieved. However, we accept when it is not.

"There have been a lot of dark forces keeping inhabitants of the human realm distracted from their paths for thousands of years. It has been a tough crusade for us to keep the light shining brighter than any darkness, so that those who are searching can see it. We have prayed for help with our missions and our prayers are being answered. There are many humans now who are allowing their light to shine brighter than ever before. They are allowing the pure greatness of I Am to shine on all they come in contact with. They are raising their awareness and thus the awareness of everyone who willingly accepts the truths of the light. The lesson of these human Angels, Earth Angels will be taught later."

"What is this you speak of? The human realm? Human Angels? Earth Angels? Where am I?"

"Quiet yourself and open yourself to all that is. The lesson of these human Angels, Earth Angels, will be taught shortly. Remember to feel and to not over think. Do not shut yourself down to this one sense when you have abundance of senses available to you. All will come to you as it is intended. When the lessons appear you will be ready."

"Please help me with a clarification: You speak of things that I do not know. I know here; I know the feelings that I feel here; I feel the beauty and completeness. I know nothing else."

"You have many questions, more than others who have recently joined us. You are not content receiving the healing energies that this Now bequeaths your soul; you seek further information concurrently. Admirable. I have been instructed to deliver you a supplementary lesson about that which you ask. Though you will receive additional communication concerning human Angels and Earth Angels in a later lesson, I will present you an impression, so that you may have clarity in your Now. The easiest way to describe Earth Angels is to say they are both human and Angel combined into one soul, a woven matrix of truths from both realms. They live in the human realm, maintain existence in a human physique, and lead a human life with all human requirements. However part of their being is of Angelic nature and composition. It is as if they have a foot in each realm, one in the human realm and the other in the Angelic realm. Because of this, they have double accountabilities, duties to perform within the human realm and duties to perform within the Angelic realm. Their sense of obligation is magnified because they are double-tasked.

"Earth Angels have a hard road to follow, a hard path to blaze for others. Their work is double because they are leading a double purpose life- a life with the purpose for a human and a life with the purpose for an Angel. Their assignment is special and Divinely charged. We pray for them and send them messages as best we can to show them that we are with them and supporting them from afar. We will leave one of our feathers for them to find. We will touch their cheek or person with a cool kiss of breeze; we will leave the same repetitive number for them to find throughout their day. It becomes a game for us really, a game with the full purpose of showing our love and support and recognition for the work they are doing.

"Though there are exceptions, many Earth Angels are not giving up or giving in when challenged or disappointed by the frailties of human nature. Instead, when facing difficulties, calling on us for help they march forward and make a difference in their own lives and, because of that, in the lives of everyone they touch. These Earth Angels have seen and have known so much more than the human realm because, you see, these Angels are accustomed to the perfection of living a life in the Angelic realm. Earth is not perfect. The human realm is not perfect. It is difficult, we know, because Earth Angels are hurt and disappointed so much. They are looked at straight in the eyes and lied to and are cheated and betrayed. They watch humans behaving in ways that are less than what they can be, what Divine sees they can be. Humans at times allow the lower energies to govern them and control them like puppets on a string. Earth Angels find themselves withdrawing more and more from the typical human-society path, to protect their hearts and to lessen disappointment, disappointment in human behavior. Because they are human, they feel hurt like humans do, especially when humans hurt one another. These beautiful service Angels work so hard to help humans see the light and be the best they can be. However, in many cases, because it is a difficult road to ward off temptations, lured by lower energies, humans falter and succumb to the path of least resistance. Being an Earth Angel is a very important role, one that is vital to the well-being of the entire universe, you see. The more light, the less dark, the more everything good and pure thrives. It is the kiss of Divine radiance. Just like you when you were a human, shining your pure light on all that you came in to contact with."

"What are you saying?" *She* shifted her thoughts, completely puzzled with the information that was just extended to her. What do you mean when I was a human? I do not remember anything but here and now; I do not have a memory of anything but this present bliss. I do not know what a human is. I am confused. I am. . ."

"Just take your time; you will have the memories that you are searching for. You will need to have those memories because you have assignments that will require you to utilize them. You did the most heroic thing that a human can do in your last life: you saved the life of another human and you did so at the expense of your own. Because of that selfless act, you were brought to us. We are in charge of teaching you and guiding you in this new way, the Angel way."

She attempted to speak, but again no words came; so again She just thought, "Angel? What you are saying? This is confusing to me? I cannot think of a life outside of this now. I do not want to, this is so wonderful."

"When we spoke to you about Earth Angels, did you not feel some connection?"

"I do not know what to feel right now. I know one thing, but now you are asking me to know another."

"You know many things; you just need to call all thoughts back to you. Take your time, they will all come."

She paused and let all thoughts come to the center. The beautiful, white light that sparkled and warmed her, made her blissful and peaceful. "But there is more." She told herself. "Bring me the thoughts that my friends speak of. Deliver me. . ."

The white light began to dissipate. The beautiful glowing images began moving away from her. Their movement was fluid and graceful as though they were floating. "Wait, please do not leave me. I do not want to be alone."

"You will never be alone. We are with you always; we are with everyone always."

"What is your name? What are all your names?"

"We do not have names; we simply have a knowingness of who we are, of who you are. We feel each other and sense each other and we all have our own sensation. We are not tethered to the independence of character and identity as humans are. We are one with all and all with one. We do have inimitable and distinct purposes and assignments. Each is linked to another and we are all for one purpose of highest good. We are all part of one. You will learn. I will feel different to you from others you will meet. You have a lot to learn, my Precious Soul; just take your time and take it in."

"Where do I go? How do I move? I do not see anyone. I am scared."

"We are with you always and forever.

Have Faith.

Think it, Feel it, Sense it

And It Is.

She relaxed and let the warmth envelope her again. The beautiful glimmering figures reappeared. "I feel you and sense you and here you are."

"You must always have faith and knowingness that we are here, even when you do not see us. When you have True Faith, you do not need things to be proven. You just *know* they are."

"Yes, I understand what you are saying. I am just confused. I do not know where we are. What I am doing here? What I am supposed to do? Where I am supposed to go? Who am I? I want to just *be,* but you tell me that there is more. I feel lost, but I feel found at the same time."

"My Beautiful Soul, you are found. You are part of the Oneness of Divine Now. Your acts of valor on earth brought you straight to us. We are here to teach you."

"When do I start?"

"You have already started. You are integrating at high frequencies at this time. All the geometric and astral truths and esoteric symbols of Divine are amalgamating throughout you. Soon you will be in complete oneness with all that is and has been and will be, just as we are. Allow this to happen seamlessly. Have patience, for there is no time here, no night or day, no past or present, it is all Now.

The past, when we recall it, is Now.

The future, when we think of it, we draw it to us,

then it is Now.

This moment is Now.

It is all Now.

"Feel the warmth and Glory of this Now and allow the process of assimilation to be completed. You will know when it is. You will be shown the steps to take when it is time. Until then just be with what is and the Now."

"Come, Beautiful Soul, it is time for you to join me now with an assignment."

"An assignment? What kind of assignment? Where are we going? What will we be doing?"

"So many questions. Quiet yourself and open yourself. All questions will be answered in due time. I have been given an assignment to lend help in the human realm, but we must move quickly. I am to take you with me to start training you for this kind of support. Stay very close to me. Move closely within my space, so that you can feel me all around you. Only concentrate on my space surrounding yours and let go of everything else."

"But where are. . ."

"Faith, Beautiful Soul. Come to me quickly now, we haven't much time."

She moved into the essence of her teacher. She could feel the effervescent warmth of her teacher surround her. Then she felt a surge of pressure, as though she were being tightly squeezed, consolidated into one small mass. The pressure increased; swirling around her so forcefully she could hear a slight buzzing noise. She wanted to call out to her teacher, but before she could, her teacher spoke, "You are safe, Beautiful Soul, Faith."

The feeling of closeness to her teacher, though foreign to her, was comforting as well. Then almost as quickly as it had begun the buzzing faded and the pressure was released. *She* could feel her teacher's essence withdraw from her. She felt a temporary void with the disconnect.

"Stay with me, Beautiful Soul. Open your senses. See what you see. Feel what you feel. Know what you instinctively know." She opened herself up. Where was She? It was familiar, but not.

"Do you know where you are? Does any of the feeling here resonate with your consciousness?"

"I do and I do not. It does and it does not."

"Open more, Beautiful Soul. This is your first assignment. See what I am seeing. Come completely to this place in this realm."

"She floated her energy of calm and faith throughout her space, her essence, allowing All that Was to be with her. Slowly her senses picked up more. She could see things materializing in front of her. Confusing, but simultaneously strangely familiar. Where are we? I cannot pull everything forward yet. All the information. . ."

"Quickly, Beautiful Soul, our assignment needs us Now, SEE."

With[1] that her senses instantly cleared and opened, She knew what she was looking at. She knew, she felt, she could see. She was inside a home, inside a room of the home, a bedroom, a child's room, an infant's room. In front of her sat a woman in a rocking chair, her head wilting to one side. The woman's eyes were closed. Her breathing was becoming heavy; she was drifting off to sleep. In her arms she cradled a new Golden Soul. The infant was sleeping as well. As She watched, She could see the woman falling deeper asleep with every breath. The glowing Golden Soul's weight was shifting. The human realm's gravity was pulling on the infant, drawing it from the safety of its loving mother's arms.

---

[1] Cross refer to real-life Angel story 1.

"Tap on the mother's shoulder," her teacher instructed. "See yourself tapping on the mother's shoulder."

Gravely concerned with the possible outcome of the situation, without hesitation, She could see her presence tapping strongly on the mother's shoulder. A deliberate tap to awaken the mother. Then She wrapped her wings around the mother and child so that they would not awaken startled and reactionary, so the mother would only arouse and regain the correct posture. She watched as the mother did just that, slowly opening her eyes, coming back to consciousness, realizing her position, and immediately correcting it, gathering the child closely to her once again. Now the mother was awake and aware. The child was safe.

"You did well, Beautiful Soul. You saved the mother and Golden Soul a fate that was not theirs to have. You instinctively wrapped your wings around them both to protect them from things that your inner sight could see. This was your first assignment. There will be more. I will not always be with you to instruct. Remember to always use your inner sight and see what it is you are to do.

"We[2] must move now, Beautiful Soul. We have an immediate calling. It gives us no time for explanation or delay. Stay with me and open all senses instantaneously, calling in all that you need. This assignment will take both of us working simultaneously. You will help the human woman and I will help the balance of humans. Hold her tightly, Beautiful Soul. Wrap your wings tightly around this human and her transference module."

"I have her, Teacher. It is difficult, because of the force of this transportation unit. It is heavy and powerful."

The massive, heavy truck flashed its right turn signal, then slowly moved its girth into the right lane, into the lane where the woman drove her small car headed to another day of work. The woman watched as the huge hunk of ominous metal slowly moved toward her. She turned her wheel to the right to avoid the beast. There was no room; a cement barrier prevented escape. Her car was trapped between the truck and the cement barrier. The woman slammed on her brakes and the giant followed suit. The shrieking of tires on the pavement teamed with the thunderous noise of the collision.

---

[2] Cross refer to real-life Angel story 2.

"Now, Beautiful Soul, move your human now! Pull her away from the large truck that is forcing itself on her. Keep the woman safe. I will direct the truck. As I push this large truck, you keep your wings locked around the woman; pull her away."

She followed her teacher's direction. The woman's vehicle was thrust away with such turbulence that She could barely keep her wings tightly gripped around the woman and her conveyance.

"Hold tightly! You must keep this human safe in her vehicle. It is not her time. We must keep all these humans safe; none must leave their path now."

She seized the vehicle tighter and with her every intention created a cushion of protection similar to a cloud around the woman, who sat clutching the steering wheel unable to move, paralyzed by fear of what was to come. The vehicle spun around and around moving as though on ice through each of the heavily occupied lanes of morning commuter traffic, as though dancing with the other cars, yet not touching one. She was there, buffering the woman from danger. She clinched her wings tighter, slowed the automobile and negotiated the landing of the vehicle, letting it hit the middle cement wall with a gentle thud and then come to rest tightly against it. Though the car hit the wall, She held it securely and had the woman blanketed in protection to prevent her injury. The other vehicles on the road screeched their brakes as the large truck and woman disengaged and followed their separate paths until they came rest. The woman sat in her vehicle facing the other cars in the lanes. The smoke from the tires billowed in the sky; the stench of rubber permeated the air. One by one, each of the vehicles in the area of the assignment came to a stop. Each vehicle was undamaged. Each vehicle had been on the wings of an Angel guiding them away from harm and safely to a pause.

"You did well, Beautiful Soul. You kept your assignment uninjured and safe from sure perils and disastrous conditions. I spread myself between the other humans on the route that morning. Dividing myself and protecting each. Did you feel how that was accomplished, Beautiful Soul?"

"Teacher, how were you able to divide yourself and come to the aid of all the humans? I felt your accomplishment, but I am unable to perceive how you provided multiple assistances."

"That is a lesson for a later point. You will be taught of the division of self and skill. One lesson at a time. You have the knowledge now that this can be done. Allow that information to converge upon your knowingness. When you are ready, more information will come to you. Just as all lessons are taught in the frame that is pre-determined for each soul."

Chapter Two

Setting the Stage

Michael pulled from under his seat the towel that he used to dust off of his new 1919 Meisenhelder Roadster. He chuckled to himself thinking of how Violet especially liked the car as they drove along with the top down, how she loved the sheen of the red and black paint and chrome, and how any bit of dust bothered her greatly as it "dampened the shine," in her words. He remembered asking her how dust could dampen a shine, but she did not change her stance. Just one of the things that he loved so much about his wife—her strong will and determination with everything.

As he brushed away the small amount of pollen that had collected on the hood, he heard someone calling his name from a distance. Looking around, Michael assessed the call as coming from a vehicle that was approaching him from the rear. He recognized the car, but barely the driver's voice over the loud rambling of car's engine. Michael raised his arm to wave at the driver but quickly recognized the expression of the driver as anything but a joyous one. The car was feet away when Michael was able to hear Randall, the yelling driver.

"Michael, you need to go," the gulping words left Randall's mouth. "It's Richard, it's the house…it's…"

Not waiting for further explanation, Michael threw his towel and himself into the roadster and motored directly to his brother-in-law's home. He did not know what was wrong, but he did know it was bad enough to take the words as well as breath from Randall, not an easy feat. As he grew closer, he could see heavy, black smoke spiraling up from the approximate location of his brother-in-law's and sister-in-law's home one street over. The street was congested with cars and pedestrians, so he pulled over and parked in front of the Dollarens' home, a half block from Richard and Natalie's home. His heart was beating so hard he could feel it in his throat as he ran in the direction of the smoke. He pushed his way through the large crowd that was already gathering around the burning house, which was indeed his relatives' home. Finally catching sight of his sister and brother-in-law, he hollered, "Natalie! Richard!"

The two were huddled together with their four boys and didn't respond. The crowd parted when they saw Michael approaching, knowing already the devastating news he was about to learn. When almost at their sides, again Michael yelled, "Natalie! Richard!"

They turned in unison in the direction of his voice. The air was clouded with dark smoke as the fire raged through the home. Their faces were wet with smoke-colored tears. "Oh, Michael, chap," Richard released the grip he had on his family and turned to embrace Michael. Natalie did the same, though her sobs made it impossible to recognize any words that she was saying.

"How could this happen? When did it start?" Michael probed.

"Oh, Michael, something terrible has happened," choked out Natalie.

"Yes, I can see. Where are the fire trucks?"
As though spurred by the question, a fire truck spun around the corner, squealing its tires. The clanging

of the bell pierced the air as it came to a stop in front of the home. "Watch out, everyone get back, make room for us," yelled a firemen. Another truck rounded the corner, the clanging bell equally as loud as the first. The spectators moved quickly to make room to the firemen. As they pulled the heavy hoses from the trucks, the chief bellowed orders.

"Do you know how the fire started"? Michael continued with his questioning.

"Chap, I think you need to sit down, in fact perhaps you need to go home. Natalie, I can stay here; would you like to take Michael. . ."

"I can't. . .I just. . .," sobbing uncontrollably, Natalie could only shake her head.

"Of course dear, you don't have to."

"Why would I need to sit, Richard? It is *your* home that is engulfed in flames. What may I do for *you*?"

"It's Violet, Michael." Natalie was finally able to form the words that she struggled to even think.

"Violet? What does Violet have to do with this?" Michael's expression turned from puzzled to shocked as he returned Natalie's and Richard's gaze. "Violet is feeding luncheon this afternoon to some of the hungry at the food-kitchen shelter. Wait? What is it? Is she here? Where is she? Tell me!" His voice became shaky as he cast his eyes through the crowd attempting to locate his wife's face.

Richard took Michael's arm, "Chap, I think we need to go sit down somewhere." By then, Richard was shaky as well, though he tried very hard to divert any attention from himself, considering the news that Michael was about to receive.

Instinctively Michael looked up at the home with its blazing hues of red, orange, and yellow in some windows and big, black smoke billowing from others. The color drained from his face and his eyes filled with tears. "Richard," he reached with his right hand and touched Richard's shoulder. "Where is my Violet? Where is my wife?" A thunderous crack from inside the home shook the ground.

"I am sorry, Uncle, sir, it is my fault. She came in for me; I am the bad one." Michael looked down at Matthew, his young nephew, comprehension dawning.

Natalie hugged her son. "You did nothing wrong, my beautiful son. I am so thankful you are alive and that your beautiful Aunt Violet was able to save you. She is an Angel now for saving your life."

"Ma'am, let me take the children," Richard and Natalie's head maid interrupted the conversation. "Ma'am, you want me to take the children?" She repeated to draw Natalie's attention.

"Yes, Emily, please take them away from here," Richard responded. "Take them to the Grosvenor Hotel. Get Luther to help you. Tell the manager who you are and why you are there."

"Richard?" Michael's patience was gone, crushed by the thoughts that were piercing his mind. His senses were caving in like the fire-ridden home in front of him.

"Michael," Natalie reached for both his hands and raised her head to look in his eyes, "your wife, my beloved sister, is gone."

Michael pulled his hands away, horrified, simultaneously knowing and incredulous. "Gone?"

Richard placed his arm around Michael's shoulder, "Chap, brother, she is inside our home."

Michael stumbled away from both of them. Dazed, he stared momentarily at the home and then thrust himself in its direction. Richard reached out for him and managed to secure his jacket, then his arm with the other hand. "It's too late. She's gone. You cannot go in there." Michael's legs buckled, his body started to spiral. Richard pulled him close to hold him up.

"What do you mean 'it's too late'? I have to go in and look for Violet." Michael twisted loose and ran to where the firemen, who, after several attempts to approach and enter the home, had begun to retreat. The heat and heavy smoke were bigger opponents than they were able to tackle.

Michael passionately pleaded with one of the fireman as he walked past, "My wife is in there; you cannot stop fighting that fire. You cannot stop, please, please do not stop, my wife. . . my Violet. . ." Michael's voice trailed off as the sobs choked his voice.

Another thunderous crash from the house and the whole second story collapsed pounding down on the first.

"Well sir, we haven't seen anyone come out. As far as we could get in, we didn't see anyone inside; there was no movement. It's just too far gone; it went up too fast to control, sir. I am sorry," reported the fireman.

Michael fell to his knees in disbelief. I cannot lose her. I cannot lose my Violet. He struggled to his feet and darted toward the home. One of the firemen grabbed his arm. "Sorry, sir, we cannot let you go in there. We cannot even make it in. It is gone, sir."

"It cannot be gone, my wife is in there. Please, just let me go. I cannot live without her." Now three firemen were constraining Michael, who with a new surge of energy, pushed and pulled in an attempt to free himself from their grasps.

A huge cracking noise from the home stilled them all, and they looked on as the whole front of the house collapsed. The crash it made was nearly deafening. "Let me go, leave me alone. I cannot leave her, I cannot live without her. I would rather go and be with her there than stay here without her."

"Michael, you cannot save her now. No one can. She is gone, Michael, the house is gone," Richard reasoned.

"How did this happen"? He fell to his knees and then lifted his head to the sky, "God, how could you do this to me"? Now hollering, "How could you take away the one person who I truly love? I cannot live without her, God. Please, please bring her back to me. Please, God, please."

By then word of the fire had spread through the town. More family members and close friends were arriving at the horrific scene. All were nearly inconsolable.

"Please tell me what I have heard is not true," moaned Marjorie, Violet's and Natalie's sister, who had just arrived on the scene. Natalie just looked at Marjorie. Without words, Marjorie knew her answer. The sisters fell in to each other's' arms and sobbed.

Colton, Michael's butler, approached, his eyes filled with tears though making every attempt to maintain his demeanor. "Sir, what would you have me do?"

Michael could barely raise his head to identify who was addressing him. Once he made eye contact, he reached his left hand toward Colton. Colton took his arm and helped Michael to his feet. "Colton, you are here? Are we missing anyone else, Colton?"

Richard intercepted he question, "We have not yet found Miss Chandra, our chambermaid, or Miss Clacie, our granny nanny."

Michael's knees buckled again. Colton firmed up his hold and kept him on his feet. By this time, the yard and front of the home had been cleared by the firemen, who moved the crowds back. The heat was searing, so most of the spectators had voluntarily chosen that option prior to being asked. Many of the townspeople watched from the street as the last of the savaged supports in the home withered to the ground. The firemen were still pouring water on the exterior in an effort to prevent the blazing inferno from spreading to other homes.

Michael straightened himself up and Colton released his grip. "Thank you Colton. Where is the rest of the staff?" "

"Sir, we heard about the fire and came as quick as we could to help. We're over here on this side; we're with Mr. Waldrip's people." Michael followed Colton, who led him to the side street where more of Richard and Natalie's staff and still more townspeople were gathered. As he walked by, people, not knowing really the proper way to address a gentleman that just lost his young, beautiful wife, mostly looked down and murmured a condolence or patted his back.

The men approached the group of employees that were huddled together weeping. When they saw Michael approaching they all straightened up, wiped their eyes, and tidied their appearances.

"Sir, how may we help? What would you like us to do?" asked the head maid.

"We are all hurting from our losses now. You do not need to think about me. Please take care of yourselves." Shifting his attention to Richard and Natalie's help, "I will make sure that you all have a room at the Grosvenor Hotel for as long as you need it. For as long as it takes us to figure out what is next."

"Sir, we just want you to know how terrible sorry we are about. . ."

Michael interrupted, not wanting to hear the words cross Colton's lips, words that would confirm the fate of his beloved Violet. "Would you all please check around the crowd to see if anyone needs help now?"

"Yes, sir."

Richard tracked down Michael again to make sure that he was not doing anything inadvisable. "Michael, what may I do for you?"

Michael looked back at Richard; a look of deep gratitude crossed his face. "My dear friend, brother, you have just lost your home and all your possessions and all you can do is check on how I am doing? Thank you, but now it is time for you to take care of your family and yourself. I have spoken with your staff and I will also speak with the Grosvenor Hotel to ensure that they have adequate accommodations for as long as is needed."

Richard was taken back by the strength he was witnessing from a man who had just lost everything that he held important in his life. "The Grosvenor, chap? All of them? Are you sure you mean the Grosvenor? The Peninsula is a fine place I understand. Much more reasonable as well."

"Yes, Richard, the Grosvenor. They have all been through too much and deserve the best. I will be taking care of this, and I do not want you to be concerned with anything. Also you and Natalie and the children will have a place with me for as long as is needed."

"Nonsense, chap, we can stay at the hotel."

"There will be no arguing these points, Richard. That is the only way that Violet would have had it, and that is the only way that it will be. Certainly I have more room than I will ever need." Michael's eyes filled with tears again and he dropped his head in somber reality.

"Thank you," is all that Richard could deliver back, as he too had again become overwhelmed with the grim reality that was thrust upon them in the last couple of hours. Together they stood staring at the flames swallowing the last of the majestic home that once monopolized nearly a quarter block, both men in a state of numbed disbelief as the town's people shuffled and mumbled around them.

Finally Michael, still staring at the crumbling home, broke the silence between the two men. "I just do not know what to do. I cannot even think of tomorrow. I cannot live without Violet. I will shrivel away. She was my everything, my morning sunshine, my afternoon laughter, my evening therapist. Tell me, Richard, what is a man to do when he loses the only thing in his life that is important to him? Why would I even get up tomorrow?" He turned and stared at Richard, his eyes empty.

Richard shook his head and then fell into an embrace with Michael, a public behavior very unlike both men, but very necessary considering the devastation each had just experienced.

"Oh my, we have been looking everywhere for you two." Marjorie and Natalie excusing their way through the crowd to join Michael and Richard, were momentarily taken aback by the sight of the two men embracing. "Come Richard and Michael, you will both stay with me. "Marjorie raised her shaking hands to gather up the men's hands.

"Actually, I believe he will be staying with us, uh, me. I have already offered our, my, home for as long as they need it," Michael interjected.

Stepping back, Richard shook his head, "I am much appreciative of your offers, but I will have to kindly decline both. We will be staying at the Grosvenor Hotel. We will need some time to ourselves to speak with the children and figure things out. I am afraid I will provide very poor company at this time as well."

"We are not concerned with the company that you will provide us. This is a time when family comes together," Marjorie responded.

"Oh, my dear sister," Michael rubbed Marjorie's arm. "I am much obliged to you for all the love you are showing me. I know it is because of the love your dear sister Violet felt for me.

Marjorie tightened her grip on Michael's hand, giving it a loving squeeze. "Dear brother, it is time for us to go."

"Excuse me, excuse me, I am Randall Kerr with the Chicago Herald. May I ask a few questions? Which one of you is Mr. Houston? How many people died in the home? How did the fire start? What. . ."

Richard stepped in front of the reporter, close enough so they could feel each other's breath. "This is not the time nor the place, Mr. Kerr. I suggest you withdraw yourself."

"Are you Mr. Waldrip and is this your home?" Then turning his head to address Michael, "Are you Mr. Houston? I heard your wife. . ."

"Perhaps I did not make myself completely clear, Mr. Kerr," Richard said leaning in even closer. "I am telling you, in no uncertain terms, that this is neither the time nor the place for you and any of your questions. I request that you leave these premises before the authorities are notified or further actions are required on my part."

"Just doing my job. I will find someone here who will talk." He turned, visually cruised the crowd, and then headed off.

"As I was saying, it is time for us to go. There is nothing more that can be done here at this time and the vultures are starting to arrive, as you can see. Please come and spend at least one night with me. I cannot manage the thought of you all being alone tonight mourning your losses. The fact in matter is that I would welcome the company myself this evening," Marjorie divulged.

"I just cannot leave. What if they find something, what if there are any questions? What if they find. . . I cannot leave her," Michael trailed off.

"This fire has several more hours before it is calm enough to be approached. Let's just go and have a sit and something to drink. Then we can come back," reasoned Marjorie.

Richard leaned in to give Natalie a kiss on her cheek and whispered in her ear, "I think it is a good idea for you to be with Marjorie. She will need help with Michael and you all will provide support for one another. None of you should be alone now. I will make sure the children are all right."

"I will need to speak with The Grosvenor Hotel to make the arrangements that we spoke of earlier, Richard," Michael interjected sensing what Richard was saying to Natalie.

"Michael, I am traveling to the Grosvenor now to check on our children. I will speak with the manager and inform him of our intentions. Nothing else need be done about this today. I suggest you escort these two beautiful women to Marjorie's home to honor them with some much needed sanctuary. You need the same too, chap."

Without resistance this time, Michael followed Violet's family away from the one thing he had known and loved the most. "I will have to dial up my family I suppose; they will need to know about this," he mumbled as he walked with the women to Marjorie's waiting car.

"Whatever you need to do, Michael, and whatever you need us to do, we are all here to help one another through this nearly unbearable situation," affirmed Marjorie.

"Raymond, please take us home now," Marjorie then directed her driver.

"Thank you, Marjorie. Violet loved you all dearly, and the love that your family members share with one another and with others has taught me how to love more deeply. Violet taught me. . ." He could speak no further; his voice cracked from the strain of the attempt. Tears once again poured down his cheeks. Struggling to clear his throat, Michael's now muffled words continued, "I am here as well to help all of you in whatever way I am able."

Settled in a bit at Marjorie's, Michael was able to compose himself and pick up the phone. "Yes, operator, I need Rochester, New York, the home of Harold Miles Houston please."

Marjorie closed the door to the study to afford Michael his needed privacy. "Barbara, please bring us tea and wafers."

"Right away ma'am, oh and, Miss McDowell, please forgive me for being so forward; but I want you to know that we all heard what happened and, well, we're just heart-broken over the whole thing. We just can't believe it and we want you to know that we are praying to God for you and your family and poor Mr. Houston. Well, I cannot even begin to know how hard. . ."

"That's enough Barbara," Marjorie snapped, then caught herself, "Thank you for your heartfelt condolences. Please bring the tea."

"Yes ma'am."

Natalie spoke, "Thank you, Marjorie, for making arrangements for the children. You are and always have been a benevolent hostess, much like Violet." With that, the two women shriveled into sobs.

"What are we to do without her? She was the backbone of this family. She organized all of us and kept us all in line too."

Lowering her voice Marjorie added, "And poor Michael. I just do not know what he will do. Their lives revolved around each another. I have never witnessed two people more in love. I was always surprised that they spent any time apart, they were so devoted to each another."

"Yes, I have the same concerns. The next few days are going to be incredibly difficult on all of us. At least having to make all the arrangements will keep him busy. It is after that period that concerns me the most; when he returns to his home that is laced with everything that she was. He will need us more than ever I fear, sister."

Chapter Three
The Discovery

T he shrill ringing of the phone silenced the conversation. Again the penetrating ring screeched through the air.

"Barbara, . ."

"Yes, ma'am, I'm getting it. The McDowell Residence."

The family sat in wait, anticipating the identity of the caller.

"Yes, operator. Kindly stay on the line while I get him." Barbara set the receiver down and shuffled to the living room entry. "Ma'am, it's for Mr. Houston." Then directing her attention to Michael, "Mr. Houston, do you want to take it?"

"Yes," Michael answered already half way to the phone. "

"This is Michael Houston."

"Yes, sheriff, I have been anticipating your call. . . Yes, Mr. Waldrip is also here at Miss McDowell's home." Michael locked eyes with Richard. "Would you prefer to speak with him first?. . Oh, can you hold a moment?"

By this time Michael was joined by Natalie, Marjorie, and Richard. All three had stiffened their postures hearing the identity of the caller. Tears permeated their eyes.

Michael removed the receiver from his mouth, "The sheriff would like to stop. . ." His voice cracked and he involuntarily let out a long, loud exhale. His hand began to shake and he lowered the phone further, this time to rest against his side to steady his grip. "The sheriff would like to speak with us in person," he pushed out before his voice could seize up again. "Would anyone object to his presence?"

Richard, who had moved to Michael's side, put his left hand on Michael's arm to help steady him.

"When Michael, this evening? Will he be joining us this evening?" questioned Marjorie.

Michael, realizing he neglected to obtain such information, raised the receiver back to his mouth, "Please excuse me for not asking, sheriff. Were you planning on joining us this evening?"

Again Michael lowered the phone, "Yes, he would like to join us this evening."

"I would welcome the information that he could bring us," Richard said. "How about you, Natalie, dear? Marjorie?"

"I agree with you, Richard," came the faint response from Natalie.

"I, as well, Richard," agreed Marjorie, turning to face Michael, "though the news he is burdened to bring us is nothing that anyone would want to receive, or deliver for that matter, in my estimation there would be no reason to put off his duty call. Are you in agreement,

Michael? Are you capable of hearing the information that he will be bringing with him this evening?"

Michael nodded and completed the call, "Yes, sheriff, this evening is amenable with everyone. Thank you, sheriff; we will look for you then."

Michael's shaky hand slowly lowered the receiver. He stood still for a few moments, his behavior not unlike the others. The news they would be receiving that evening was nothing that anyone could prepare for. Even the most callous of persons would find it difficult to grasp and internalize news of such horrific magnitude. They silently began to ready themselves as best as could be imagined and awaited the news that they both did and did not want to hear.

The knocking on the door, though expected, made each jump. "I got it, ma'am," delivered Barbara as she moved to the door. "Please come in, sheriff and Mr. . .uh. . .may I take your hats?"

"Thank you. I am Sheriff Ronald Newton and this is Deputy Martin Shields. We are here to speak with Miss McDowell, Mr. and Mrs. Waldrip, and Mr. Houston."

"Yes sir, they have been expecting you. Please follow me."

"Miss McDowell ma'am, this is the Sheriff Newton and Deputy Shields."

"Thank you, Barbara."

"Gentlemen, please come in and make yourselves comfortable. Let me introduce myself. I am Miss Marjorie Elizabeth McDowell." Marjorie led the men into the living room. "This is my sister, Mrs. Natalie Ashley Waldrip and her husband Mr. Richard Nathaniel Waldrip, and this is my sister's. . .my brother-in-law, Mr. Michael Thomas Houston."

"It is nice to meet you all. Thank you for welcoming us in to your home, Miss McDowell and allowing us the opportunity to speak with you all in person. I am Sheriff Ronald Newton and this is Deputy Martin Shields."

"Please gentleman, be seated."

"Thank you kindly."

"May I offer you something to drink? Coffee, tea, perhaps something stronger?" Marjorie gestured to a lavish table indicating there was more to offer than coffee or tea and hobbled in its direction. She had been born with one leg shorter than the other, which caused her to walk with a limp, something she had been self-conscious of all her life.

"Marjorie," scolded Natalie knowing that offering a libation to a law enforcement officer during prohibition could create a situation of its own, one which none of them would want to be associated with.

"The information that these poor gentleman must give to us this evening may flow much easier with something stronger than tea or coffee, my dear sister."

"Thank you, Miss McDowell, but, no, we are on duty and do not need anything to drink. Though, thank you kindly for the offer of coffee and tea.

"You are correct with your assessment. The information that we must share with you is what we wish, when we enter this line of work, we never have to share. Sirs, madams, I will approach this as best I know how, by giving you the facts of the case as we know them now."

"Thank you, sheriff, we are prepared, as best we can be, considering," acknowledged Richard.

"As you know, Mr. and Mrs. Waldrip, your home has been lost in the fire. The firemen were unable to save anything. The home was nearly fully engulfed by the time the first firemen arrived and try as they might, their hoses were no match for the inferno that met them. They were able to limit the spread of the fire. Neighboring homes either were untouched or suffered minor damage, discoloration, heat damage, and the like, which is really a miracle."

"Sheriff, my wife and I appreciate your assessment of our home. We are, however, more consumed with the. . .well. . .with the other ravages associated with the fire."

"Yes, yes, I understand, Mr. Waldrip." Clearing his throat and shifting his gaze, "Mr. Houston, it pains me to be the bearer of such news. I have rehearsed its delivery in my head since I realized I would be the one here this evening, but I find no good way to share the information."

Michael's head dropped and he began to sob in anticipation to what he was about to hear. He had secretly been holding off reality in hopes that his wife would somehow miraculously be found alive. The sheriff's demeanor now dispelled that illusion. Natalie moved to his right side and clutched his hand. She, too, was unable to control her emotions. Marjorie, who sat directly across from them, who was generally of stoic disposition, collapsed on the side arm of the sofa, weeping. Richards's eyes, red and worn from the day, filled with tears that rolled silently down his cheeks as he attempted to maintain eye contact with the sheriff.

"When I arrived at the blaze this afternoon, I was told that there were possible, well, missing persons. Though it is difficult at this point to make any positive identifications, I must tell you that we have located three bodies in the rubble."

The volume of the weeping from the women intensified. Although Violet's family was prepared to hear the anticipated report, how can anyone completely prepare when they have to hear the news that they have lost a loved one, especially in such an unimaginable way.

Michael raised his head; his eyes were swollen and bloodshot. Tears continued to flow as he worked hard to maintain his dignity. "Thank you, sheriff. We recognize that the information you have to share with us this evening is none too easy. We know," he instinctively tightened his grip on Natalie's hand, "my wife, Mrs. Violet Houston, is one of the persons lost to the fire. It is my understanding as well that she reentered the home a second time, missioned with saving some of the family help. Is that your understanding?"

"Mr. Houston, I cannot speak to your wife's intent, as heroic as it may have been, because I was not present at the time. I can, however, confirm that the bodies found were adults. I again must add that we have not attempted to make positive identification at this time."

"Yes, sheriff, that we understand. It is with logic that we can all draw the same conclusion: if three are missing and there were three bodies recovered, then no further investigation need be done," Richard deduced.

"Yes sir, I do agree with you. One of the bodies was found at the rear of the home. Though I was never in your home, by various kitchen items present, it appeared to be in the kitchen. Two bodies were found at the front of the home, approximately three to four feet from the front door. These bodies were side-by-side."

Michael dropped his head and try as he might, could not control his sobs. The reality that his beloved could very well have been just inches from escape made it even more difficult to endure the already agonizing news. His mind ran rampant. If he had only tried to get close enough to attempt a rescue. If he had only pushed through the heat and flames, perhaps he could have saved her. Perhaps he could have. . .

As though knowing Michael's thoughts, Marjorie broke the temporary silence, "It will do no good attempting to recreate the events of this afternoon. It will benefit nothing and will only prolong our inescapable pain. We have lost our beloved sister, your beloved wife, Michael. Natalie and Richard, you have lost two of your faithful wait staff, your magnificent home, and all your possessions. If it had not been for our dear sister, Violet, you would be mourning the loss of your son, Matthew, as well. She is Matthew's Angel. We are all feeling deep agony and I am sorry for all of us. The loss today has been catastrophic. We all need to take our time to heal and move forward. Reliving the event will do no good."

"You are right, my wise sister," Natalie squeezed Michael's hand. "We must all work hard at healing the pain. Richard and I can rebuild. No one need worry about that. Let us all concentrate on helping one another through this difficult time for the sake of our dearly departed benevolent sister, Violet. We cannot let her life and actions go unrecognized. We need to honor her actions. She saved the life of our son, Matthew, and she attempted to save Chandra and Clacie as well. This act of heroism needs to be celebrated. And, we need also to try to extend some comfort to Chandra's and Clacie's families."

Richard stood, which prompted the other three men to do the same. "Thank you, sheriff, deputy. Again we appreciate your delivering this difficult news in person. None too easy a task and we respect your decision to do it. I believe we will all need time to process the information, information that not a one of us dreamt of twenty-four hours ago. If you would be so kind as to continue to update us with any news, we would all be greatly appreciative,"

"Thank you again for welcoming us in to your home, Miss McDowell."

"It was an honor meeting you, Mr. Waldrip," The sheriff reached his hand out to shake Richard's and Richard responded in like manner.

"Mr. Houston, I wish to express my heart-felt sympathy for your loss. May God grant you some kind of sanctum for your recovery. For all your recoveries." He looked to each and then extended his hand to Michael and shook it long and hard, patting his shoulder with the other hand. As the men looked steadfastly at each other, Sheriff Newton chased away thoughts of having to survive the same type of ordeal with his wife, Marie.

"My sincere condolences," Deputy Shields extended his hand to Richard and then to Michael. "Ladies, may God grant you the serenity of your prayers."

"Thank you, deputy," the sisters responded in unrehearsed unison.

"Let me show you out," Richard gestured with his right hand toward the front door.

"Thank you. Good night, all."

Barbara stood at the threshold of the hall, "I got it from here, Mr. Waldrip, sir. You join your family now. You all need each other. Sheriff, deputy, this way; I'll get your hats."

The crackling of the wood in the large fireplace that graced the room was the only sound echoing against the walls. Richard stood staring at the front door for a moment before turning to join the rest. His thoughts jetted from one aspect of the devastating event to the other. The ramifications were certainly long reaching.

"Richard, what of our children? Shouldn't we check on them, go to them now?" Natalie sniffled through her question.

"Please bring your children and stay here with me. There is plenty of room in this huge old home, and it would do us well to all be together."

"We have already relocated the children and the help there, so for now we will stay there until things settle. We have a fairly large group, as you know. "

"Richard, Natalie, you know I have plenty of room for your help too; half the town's help at that. There is no reason to stay elsewhere."

"Thank you, Marjorie. That is something we can revisit tomorrow. I am too tired to consider making any more decisions at this time. Richard, I feel I need to get to the children now, especially Matthew. I am sure that he is..." she stopped unable to continue any words that revolved around the painful event.

"Yes, dear. I believe you are right. It is time to retire to the Grosvenor and our children." Richard walked to where Natalie and Michael sat, still mindlessly clinging on to each other's hands. Richard extended his hand to Natalie to help her rise. Michael stood as well. The men again, without word, fell into embrace holding the grip and hugging for a long minute. Pulling away, Richard looked at Michael with tear- drenched eyes. "Chap, I will be by in the morning. You are, of course, staying here with Marjorie tonight. There is nothing we can do until then. Please try to get some rest." He patted Michael's shoulder.

Marjorie and Natalie, too, fell into each other's arms weeping again despite their best efforts at controlling it.

"Thank you, my dear sister, for hosting us this evening. Thank you for taking care of Michael. I love you Marjorie."

"I love you, Natalie. Together we can be strong."

Richard gave Marjorie a hug too; something that rarely happened.

"Oh my, you will need a wrap, Natalie. There might be a chill in the air tonight. Barbara, please see that Natalie has one of my wraps; perhaps the beautiful long white one. Good night to you both."

Marjorie and Michael looked at each other. The fire cracked and popped in the new silence of the room. "I am going to make myself a cocktail, Michael. Will you join me?"

"Yes Marjorie, I believe I will join you."

Chapter Four

The Lessons of Soul's Image

and

Conflicts of Character

"I can remember him, but I can't. I can see his face, his image. Who is he? He is so familiar to me, but unfamiliar at the same time. Is that what humans are, familiar and unfamiliar at the same time? "

"Yes it is, as though you know them, but you do not really know them."

"You are new to me. I feel you are different from the last Angel that I spoke with. Is that true? Are you my new teacher?"

"Yes, Beautiful Soul, I am your new teacher. You will have different teachers for different lessons, depending on your needs and the requirements of the assignments. You will learn many lessons for assignments. All assignments are different; however, they have one common thread- we will be aiding the human realm with cases that have fallen off the track of their pre-designated course."

"I do not understand your meaning, Teacher? Cases that have fallen off track of their pre-designated course? What is this that you speak of?"

"The human realm has many variables and complexities that humans keep hidden and only upon occasion show others. That is why many humans feel confused around other humans whom they think they know. One cannot hold an assortment of different pictures of oneself and present a picture to others based on the image that one believes those others would like to see, holding back the true picture of one's soul for fear that another will not like the actual soul picture. When one does this, one becomes confused about which picture has been shown to whom and confused themselves about who they really are. You see, souls are expecting to meet the energy they *feel* other people are; and, when they are shown a picture of someone else, the picture conflicts with what they feel, attracting that conflicted energy to the viewer and back to the one projecting the inaccurate image. Others cannot see the truth of the soul clearly when this is done. The ones showing the incorrect pictures of themselves are now in a position of not seeing themselves clearly, because they have pulled forward in themselves the conflicts of character. The lesson of great importance is that each soul, no matter the vessel they are transported in, must always be true to the genuine soul's image. The lesson is to show others who they truthfully are without judgment of themselves; without criticism, or embarrassment, without any of the lower emotions that distract one from the Divine wonder that they are. One must always be true to one's self.

"Some of these inconsistencies of character can also be attributed to the fact that some humans have attached themselves, corded themselves, to other humans. When this is done, they are giving others their energy and they are taking energy from the ones they have corded. When this cording happens, humans cannot operate at their full potential because they do not have all their own energy and the balance is filled with other energies that do not have the same missions in life as their own energy has. In the case of attachments and cording, humans, for the most part, are unaware that they are carrying the matrix of truth from another human. Though the awareness of pure self has begun, many humans are still disconnected from the truths that are their own, the truths that are woven into their being for each individual lifetime.

"You see humans have learned to live with closed hearts and souls. They do this out of self-protection. They do this for the most part because they have not learned yet how to give pure love without being hurt or feeling vulnerable. This creates numbness in them.

These are all lessons that we are tasked to share and teach. Some lessons are given to humans via experiences in their lives. Unfortunately, we have found that many do not learn from the lessons they are given through experiences. Instead, they feel victimized. Instead of having the belief that everything that comes to them is for their greater good to help them accomplish what they need to accomplish in this lifetime, they begin holding onto negative aspects and emotions. They turn a lesson into a knife that they use on themselves. We must help these humans to value the lesson as an opportunity for advancement. There is no harm in a lesson when it is received as so."

"I can feel what you are saying is true. I can remember what you are saying as a feeling, as though I have felt this before."

"Few humans have not felt this. The enlightened beings are aware of this. Every soul returning to human form does so with its own matrix of truth, truth of being and purpose for a lifetime. Children are born with their own individual truths for their being. Sadly, more times than not, they are moved away from their path and onto the paths of others. This is a very important awareness that we are working hard to insert into the knowingness of humans now. Humans must begin supporting one another's growth and path. The time of conformity and convergent thinking and acting must end. The truth of how this action of steering souls off their own paths and onto the paths of others must be illuminated. In doing so, it will become painfully obvious how this process has stifled growth and in some cases even reversed it. When the practice of supporting a child's purpose from birth on is embraced and practiced, then the accomplishments and advancements in mind, body and soul will be limitless. Completeness will be felt on heaven and on earth. You will have another lesson on this important process and you will help with this, Beautiful Soul."

"How will I help? How are humans being taught this lesson?"

"Patience and Faith in this Now, Beautiful Soul. Let us stay with this important lesson of Soul's image and the conflicts of character."

"Yes, Teacher. I apologize for disrupting the valued lesson."

"There is yet another important reason to teach you why humans display inconsistencies in their behavior and personality. Many humans are controlled by False Realness. Many dark shadows hide behind false faces of good. Earth has been covered by a cloak of negative lower energy that is hiding behind a mask of good. The earth has been drenched for eons with this bitterly toxic-waste energy, pulling human souls down deeper and deeper into the spoil. These lower and negative energies attracted humans with false illusions of what was deemed good in many areas of human life. Past leaders of lands and kingdoms, who once held prestigious positions and were much revered, fell in part due to the fact that the once the pure souls of the leaders were courted by negativity, they held the mirror on others and not themselves.

"Once the negative energy attaches itself, it will stay, creating unwanted chaos until the human has the awareness of a presence or behavior that is unwanted. The person will then take measures to rid the negative involvement. The new evolution of higher consciousness thinking and acting is pulling human souls—in higher numbers than we have rejoiced in before—out from under the cover of the devastation caused by this cloaking of negativity. This negative energy is not to be feared or troubled about as it can be corrected once the awareness has been made. It is simply an explanation of what has been and an aspect we are helping the human realm become aware of and move away from in order to take steps to higher consciousness.

"There is much that we are helping with simultaneously in an effort to sponsor the increased cognizant eye. Every human spirit is being cleansed and many do not know it. They just know that things are moving faster, things seem or feel different. Many realms are involved in this earth and human realm cleansing. It is as though an Angel's Wing were wiping through the soul of all, a spray of water from an Angelic power washer is rinsing off humans and this earth. The Divine vibrations, the frequencies of everything are rising. When the vibration of higher consciousness rises, the lower and negative energies cannot hold on. They fall off and are washed away. The higher the awareness, the more good is absorbed. The higher the Divine vibration that humans and the earth vibrate in, the better able they are to communicate with the higher frequencies and higher realms in the universe. Things are very charged now because everything is making a shift to this higher vibration. Involvement in this mass cleansing is making tired even the unknowing, those who have not opened themselves to the truths of the current shift, which, as taught, is larger than any shift in time.

"Knowing what is coming and then feeling when it is integrated, the souls that choose to be involved in the happening will experience an almost euphoric shift,. Their job is not an easy one, and they will be challenged to new heights of involvement in the coordinated effort of the universe to help earth and the human realm, knowing that in helping these two, all realms are helped. In rebellion to the high charge, the lower and negative energies will be in an uproar as they feel the cooperative effort to raise operations above a level at which that they are able to function. However, because of the increased number of humans advancing their conscious level of thinking, those destructive energies are losing this time. The light is being shined upon them and they are being seen for what they are and not for the illusion they have fostered in the past.

The souls that choose to join the human realm with this advanced mission of heightened awareness are much admired and appreciated by many jurisdictions. It is the largest shift that the world has been through. It is not an easy task that they embark upon; that fact is known collectively. Some souls come into a human life with a special mission: to do prep work for this cleansing and advancement modification. Once they have completed their preparation task for this time in Now, they will excuse themselves, while the job of removing, releasing, and enhancing proceeds. In addition, there are some souls in human form that are unable to operate at this high pace during the shift to higher frequency; they will opt to leave the earth for now. Once the integration is complete, there will be a sense of calm in the realm. These souls may determine there will be purposes for their administering and completion then. Do you comprehend the invaluable contents of this lesson?"

"Yes teacher, what you share gives great insight into the many variables that humans must endure. It gives me appreciation for their determination through strife and suffering. It is truly humbling to witness the cooperative effort involved in aiding the human realm in their much needed advancement. When will I begin my lessons on how I am to help?"

"Oh, Young Soul, you are learning Now. Feel around you. You are surrounded by others learning Now. You will have many lessons, many classes. You will learn what you need to know for your next assignment, just as those around you are learning."

She felt around her and realized that She was surrounded by other lights, all twinkling and glowing joyously, eagerly learning the lessons being taught.

She also sensed a new prominent presence. "You are a new teacher to me."

"Yes, New One, and now the lesson continues. We are constantly teaching the human realm. We of the Angelic realm help humans remember the truths that they were born with by creating learning experiences in their current human life to jar this information forward to light from where they have kept it hidden. You see, many humans hide their truths and purposes for fear of ridicule, for fear of being bullied or made fun of for being different. They believe that if they are all the same and do not bring attention to themselves, then they will not be hurt. So, they hide away their own truth of being and adopt one that they think will be society acceptable, feeling safe from being different from the norm. However, deep in their being they know that they are not living the life that they were designed to live and because of that, they can never achieve complete happiness, the happiness that comes when a purpose is fulfilled, when a truth is respected and supported. When, despite the consequences, they allow the true meaning of their life to shine and they follow their paths to accomplish the things that they themselves chose to do in their lifetime, true happiness and even euphoria will be experienced.

"Every being in the universe has the seed of knowledge that it takes All to accomplish One. No matter how small one's purpose is and how large another's is, it is with the fulfillment of each purpose that we all are able to move into complete enlightenment and co-create a Divine for all."

"How do we do this? How may we help humans see the beauty that they possess and how can we help them see that their beauty is no less than anyone else's, that their truths and purpose are no less important than anyone else's, and that their truths and their purposes are vitally important to the wholeness of all?"

"Young Soul, you are filled with beautiful light and your question reveals that you have learned this portion of the lesson well. You now *feel* the importance of helping with individual recognition of purpose. We have groups that help with these lessons. They enter the human realm and provide lessons to remind a soul of the divine messages that they brought with them to share and goals to accomplish. You will go with a guide to observe this important work."

"When? When will I go? What will I do?"

"Remember to feel. When you feel, then you sense all that is and was and will be. You will sense when and what you should do. Unfortunately, humans are taught to doubt their feelings. We understand that the humans will receive a message and then doubt its origins, often times thinking the message is something that they just imagined or thought up themselves. They spend a lot of time proving why things cannot be, instead of believing that things are. They allow the over analyzing of messages that we send to them until the true meaning of the message is gone. This is another large lesson that we are trying to teach the human realm: the realization that they need to honor the messages they receive, since the messages are sent with Divine purpose. Some are not used to the different platforms that we use to deliver messages. We send messages in different ways. This is something that you will learn more of when the time is right.

"It is a tediously simple task we have to help the human realm with learning to receive messages. To us, the idea that humans should immediately understand and embrace the messages we send them, especially when they have asked us for help, seems natural because we send the messages with love and good intentions to help. It should be a simple thing for them to receive and accept. It is a basic assignment. However, this has proven to be a much bigger task than any expected. Centuries laden with doubt and fear have engulfed the human realm so that restraining the negatively charged side effects of these emotions is proving to be quite problematic because the tentacles have deep reaches in society, where doubt is accepted.

"The humans who do not have enlightened thinking will dismiss all messages as thoughts from their imagination, mostly because when they hear a message, it is in their own voice. As humans allow their conscious levels to elevate, they are able to discern the messages that are sent to them from their own thinking. They release doubt from their inventory of emotions and embrace the Faith that all things can be that are.

"We have a large army of Angels on earth helping with this shift. You, too, will go and help a human soul with this increased knowingness."

"I do not remember this human trait that you speak of; yet I am to help in the human realm to cure it?"

"Beautiful Light, open yourself up to the pattern of what is in the Now."

"I feel you are new to me. Are you my new teacher?"

"Yes, Beautiful Light, I am."

"I feel much softness from you. You feel so warm and gentle to me."

"You do know this human trait. You were a human so you have experienced this either within yourself or in some around you at the time. Open yourself up to receiving the information."

"I do not remember. I just know what is now. I do not know much of what humans are. I cannot remember being a human. This is confusing to me. Why do I not know anything of what you speak? Why do I only know what is here and now? . . . I just thought I remembered something, something that was familiar to me. An image different from us. The image made me feel loved, but then it made me very sad. And then the image was gone."

"You will remember, Beautiful Light. The memories will come to you when you are ready, but not until you are ready to receive them and view the movie of your human life. You simply are not ready to have all the memories come to you yet. There is a lot to learn here. All will happen as it needs to, when it needs to. Do not rush or worry. It is all what it is, how it is. There is no rush, because there is no ending time. It is limitless, as are we, as are you. Just allow yourself to be and fill yourself with the love that is pure, accepting, eternal. Do not think now. Just accept the oneness of I Am."

D ressed[3] in his finest, though entirely unmindful of it, Michael escorted his sister-in-law, Marjorie, by the arm through the heavy wooden doors of the church. Behind him followed Richard and Natalie and their sons, Michael's family who traveled to join him as well as some of Violet's extended family and both families domestic staff. This was the first time the family had all been out since the horrific fire. They and the majority of the town came together to lay Violet to rest. Michael began to opt for a pew in the back of the church, but Marjorie steered them forward to the first row in the front. Michael stood and allowed the families to advance in past him and take their seats, while he remained at the aisle end of the pew.

Very aware that all eyes were on him and his family, biting his inner lip to prevent the tears from welling in his eyes, he stoically stared straight ahead, controlling his thoughts, fighting off the numbing despair that he had come to know as commonplace. He could hear the murmuring voices behind him but intentionally avoided listening to what they might be

---

[3] Cross refer to real-life Angel story 3.

saying. The truth was he did not feel strong enough to hear what they might be saying.

As the priest moved to the podium, Michael felt a hand on his shoulder. He reluctantly turned his head to acknowledge the deliverer, assuming it was a church-goer wishing him well. There was no one at his side. He turned his head and looked at the row behind him. His look was returned with a somber smile of condolence. Michael tipped his head in appreciation. As he turned his head back toward the alter, he stopped, instantly immobilized, his eyes frozen. Before him stood his Violet; she smiled at him in the loving manner that had always taken his breath away. He gasped.

Marjorie reached for his arm, "Are you all right? she whispered.

Michael turned to her. "It is. . ." turning back toward Violet, his voice trailed off. Violet was not there. He turned and looked back down the aisle between the rows of pews. He saw her again, though she was transparent, a cloudy, wispy figure floating toward the back of the church. Michael watched as she gently and lovingly touched the attendees on the shoulder along the way and then evaporated before his eyes. He could do nothing but stare in disbelief. What had he seen? *Was it Violet? Did she come back to see him one last time?*

Marjorie again grasped Michael's arm, "Are you all right? What is it?" Michael's eyes caught the eyes of all the attendees sitting behind them. They were all staring at him in an inquisitive manner. Realizing how his actions must look, he slowly turned his head forward and sat motionless, unable to speak, mesmerized by his vision, confused by what he thought that he had seen. Perhaps the nights of no sleep coupled with his tragic loss had robbed him of rational judgment, had made him light-headed. His mind was full, but he could not reflect; he could not bring logic to what he had just witnessed. He let his head drop to his hands and despite his desire to maintain composure, he sobbed. How could one person miss another so much?

"I remember my life with this human, I see him now. He is my love. He is Michael, he is my husband. I remember. He is my husband, Michael. We love each other. Why am I not with Michael? I miss him."

"Yes, Beautiful Soul, it was time for you to remember things from your human life so that you may aid the souls you left with their closure and help them to move forward. Humans must understand that the passing of a human body is just the removal of the soul from one physical embodiment to another space. When a human's soul transfers from the life they piloted to the next stage for that soul, the humans staying behind who were touched by the transferring human must continue forward. They must satisfy their own purposes for leading a human life." It is an important message for all humans to know.

"I remember more with Michael now. The fire, my sister's home, Richard and Natalie's home. Oh! Chandra and Clacie—I could not find them. I only found Matthew. I could not see. The air was so thick. I was choking, coughing, I could not breathe. I was trying to call out, but I was coughing. I fell to my knees. I was crawling, feeling with my hands, trying to recognize where I was in the home; feeling for something familiar. I needed to find the door. I was crawling as fast as I could. My eyes burned so I kept them tightly closed. I felt a door. I had made it. I reached feeling for the door handle. Where was the handle? I could not feel it. The smoky air burned my lungs, burned my throat. It felt like my esophagus was on fire. I took short breaths. I ripped off a section of my dress and wrapped it around my head and reached for the door handle again. But it was not there. I needed to get outside, I needed fresh air. I felt something. It was the hinge. The hinge was on the wrong side; the door handle should be there. I had the wrong door. It was not the entry door. It was a different door. I think, think. . .it was the kitchen door. I went the wrong way. I needed to turn around, crawl towards the front door, to exit the home. The smoke was too hot. I could not breathe. My head was dizzy. I fell over. I fell against something. What was it? I could not think clearly. 'Get up...get up...move forward.' I told myself. I was so tired. The air was gone. I lay on my stomach and tried dragging myself. With my left arm I reached forward and grasped the rug and pulled myself forward. My head dropped to the ground and knocked me awake again. I tried drawing air in through my mouth. It was so hot, so thick. I do not remember anymore. I, I cannot remember what happened." She gasped, "That is why I am here. I died in the fire. I didn't get out. Did Clacie and Chandra get out? Were they lost in the blaze as well? It saddens me greatly to think of them dying." How many lives did the fire take?

"Calm yourself, Beautiful Light, calm yourself. Look at where you are. Nothing is ever lost. All is how it is supposed to be. Some human souls leave the earth plane before others. Their jobs are done. All souls have assignments, as we have discussed, that they take with them to their human life. Their assignments are intertwined in the matrix of their being. Just like DNA. They are the pure truths of each being when the being enters its life. The purposes of their entry to the human realm are their Truth of Being. Some souls have long assignments and some have short. It is all how it is supposed to be. There is no end. There is just a new beginning, a new chance to make a difference somewhere. Look at your human life as an example. You had assignments to accomplish, which you did. More than just your predetermined truths, you stepped into a position of making a universal difference when you chose to save the life of Matthew and the others over the risk of losing your own life. As you were told before, that is an undeniable heroism that is recognized here in this realm. To put your life below the importance of another's is something that is never asked for or expected. We would never expect someone to take a human life form and then donate it to save another. Despite this, there are a few human souls that are so selfless that they never consider themselves when stepping in to save another. These souls, like you, are graced with special purpose for enlightening the universe. Like you, we elevate these souls to assume roles of Divine Grace. Many souls will enter the human realm lifetime after lifetime on the mission of achieving their truths. However, there are a few souls that demonstrate a self-sacrificing quality that is revered. Such as you, Beautiful Light. Unless it is your desire, you will not reenter the human realm as a human. You will return as an Angel, providing Angelic guidance and assistance as needed."

"I miss my husband, I miss Michael. Will I ever see him again? I want only good for him."

"Calm yourself, Beautiful Light, as I have said before, All is as it should be, as it needs to be. Your human Michael still lives the life you knew him in. Your family all live that same life as well. It is not their time to leave that life. They still have their own assignments to achieve." As you become progressively more integrated into the Angelic realm, the feelings of loss that you experience will leave you as the recognition of the important process of soul evolution identifies itself to you.

"It makes me happy to hear you say those words. Thank you for sharing that with me. Who lost their life as I did?"

"Again, Beautiful Light, no one lost their life. Each has simply moved from one existence to another. Their human names in the life you remember were Chandra Jodie Sause and Clacie Adisynn Owens. Both have already reentered the human realm with new truths for their being."

"How could they have reentered the human realm already? How was there time for them to? I have only been here a short period. I have done nothing yet."

"You have learned much. It is easy to be confused when the information presented to you is foreign. As I have schooled you, unless by choice, you will not reenter as a human. Both those souls have new human lives with new missions for accomplishment. They are happy to graduate to new levels, and we are happy that they did. You see, some humans are unable to remember the truths they took with them to their human life. When a human does not learn the lessons they are supposed to learn in a lifetime, then they will be tasked with the same assignments until they are able to master them."

"Are you saying some humans have to repeat their lives to learn the same lessons?"

"Yes, sadly, that is what I am telling you. They do not return to the same vessel they lived in before, or the same life just lived; they return to the human realm in new vessels in a new life, but with the same purposes and missions to accomplish as the last life. There is no progression for these souls only a repeat of assignments. Because of the lower energies that are filled with distracting maneuvers, some humans are kept diverted from their path for the better part of their lives, sometimes all their lives. So the valuable lessons they were to learn and share with others were not accomplished. When humans do not follow the path they entered their life to follow, it creates a delay in progress; they are unable to achieve the needed advancement. Due to the enormous number of uncompleted duties, advancements have been atrophied not only on earth, but universally. We need to help humans remember why they entered the life they are living. We need humans to help humans with this mission, to support one another with their individual tasks, and accept the fact that everyone is separate in task, but connected in outcome. The Angelic realm can provide assistance; but because of humans' free will, it cannot step in unless a human asks for help."

"We can never step in?"

"There are exceptions to this rule. If a human is in danger and the situation is not part of their truth matrix, then an Angel can step in and help. Generally it is the human's Guardian Angel that performs this rescue, unless the task is more than the Guardian Angel is able to perform. In that case, a Guardian Angel will request the aid of another Guardian. And, sometimes Earth Angels can create miracles that we cannot. There are different levels in the Angelic realm, but that is a lesson for a different time."

"I am quite concerned with Master Houston, ma'am," Barbara lowered her voice to confide her feelings to Marjorie, as she poured her a cup of tea. "He is barely eating still. Well, it's been nearly three weeks since the passing; he is gonna make himself sick, if he doesn't take better care of himself."

"Thank you, Barbara. Yes, I agree with you. I have my concerns about him as well. Though every time

Page 89

I address the subject with him he passes if off as nonsense. He is a stubborn man, that one."

"Yes, ma'am, I tried fixing some of my best dishes for him, thinking it would tempt him to eat more, but he just doesn't."

"Thank you for caring for him as you do. I guess that is all anyone can do right now. . .and allow time for the pain and the deep wounds to heal. Our family has been dealt quite a card. Only God knows why. We must keep our faith and our chins up and trust in the Lord to lead us on the path of healing. Has Mr. Houston been down yet today?"

"No ma'am, he's still up in his room. He spends so much time there, it is troubling, but I guess we can only do what we can do, like you say ma'am. The last time he went out of the house was to church that Sunday and he hasn't been back since."

"True."

"It's like something happened to him when he went to church; something is different. Despite what you have said, I still believe something happened to him in church that day, ma'am. He just seemed spooked when he got home."

"That is enough of that kind of talk. Let's move the conversation on, please."

"Yes ma'am. According to Colton, I understand that Miss Natalie and Master Richard's new place is being started. Not all too soon either. They're all growing quite tired of the hotel."

"Yes, I can imagine they are. Barbara, I neglected to mention that Natalie will be stopping by this afternoon for tea. It will be nice to see her. I have not spoken with her in nearly five days. She is all consumed with attempting to create some kind of normalcy for her children and husband. That Richard, he is such a good man and has been such a pillar for all of us through this. So much Natalie has on her plate, not to mention her own grief and all the planning she has to undertake for the new home. So many items have to be ordered from abroad and will take months to arrive. The Grosvenor is taking wonderful care of them; but, as you say, a hotel never really feels like home.

"I will be going out late morning and will return early afternoon before my sister arrives. Please let them know to have the car ready for me at eleven, Barbara. I have a few items I must address. If I miss Michael, please inform him of the plans. Now I need a little time to read."

"Yes, ma'am."

A[4] small stream of light made its way through a crack in the heavy velvet draperies that hung floor to ceiling across the massive windows in the room were Michael slept. His eyes focused on the light and then on how it illuminated items across the noble room. The reality of his location and position never left him. Since he lost his beloved wife, he had not been back to his own home except to collect some personal effects. He dreamt of his Violet. He woke thinking of her. The pain of his loss still overwhelmed his every sense and was nearly unbearable. Tears rolled down his cheeks as memories of their honeymoon flowed over him. Michael was covered and clouded with grief and loneliness. How could he possibly wake every day missing someone so badly? How could he go on with his own life? There were times when his mind would slip off to

[4] Cross refer to real-life Angel story 4.

dark places, to thoughts that were, at the time, all consuming. The sadness and loneliness permeated his being, sending him on a downward tail spin to places that he feared, somber spaces that brewed hopelessness and despair. He was overcome with thoughts of worthlessness and defeat, as though he had nothing to offer anyone and, if he did, no energy to deliver it. Nothing in his life was important anymore. He felt he had no reason to live. All he wanted to do was stay in bed curled up in a fetal position and sleep—forget about everything, all the stress, all the pain, all the feelings of complete void and insignificance, hoping that sleep would wash away reality and he would wake to see it was all a dream.

Sitting up in bed, he mumbled, "If only there was some way, my darling Violet, that you could show me a sign that you are all right. If you could speak to me or touch me. Just one sign, my darling." He glanced around the room. There were several table lamps and floor lamps in the room. "All right, my darling, if you are all right, would you just communicate with me through this lamp, this lamp sitting on this nightstand. If you are there, if you are all right, would you make the lamp turn off— make the light bulb go out?" He turned on the lamp with a sense of apprehension. He sat for a few minutes staring at the lamp; nothing happened. He let out a long sigh and rested his back against his pillows. "What did I think would happen," he mumbled to himself. "She is gone. She cannot communicate with me; that is impossible." Just as the last word trailed from his mouth, the light went off, untouched and unprovoked. He gasped not sure that he did indeed see what he had just seen. He looked to see if perhaps the bed had giggled the stand; they did not touch each other. Wonderment encompassed him. "Violet, my darling Violet, thank you for coming to me and for showing me this sign. I miss you every day and I love all that you are and were to me. It does my heart good to know that you are safe and in a good place. Thank you, darling."

Then Michael felt a breeze by his ear and words entered his mind as though they were being whispered to him, "It is time for you to begin living again, my darling husband. You are much too young to be so alone. You have too much to give to this world, and you can no longer keep yourself secluded. You must live. You must do this for your family, for all who will benefit from meeting you, for yourself, and, my darling husband, for me. I will always love you and I will always be a part of you, but you can no longer remove yourself from the very world that you are dedicated to help; you can no longer be selfish with yourself."

As quickly as the breeze had come to him, it was gone. The message lingered and swirled around him

Page 94

almost making him dizzy. He knew it was his Violet. He could feel her warmth, her pure heart of love caring for him and those around him even after she passed. Violet was right. It was time to begin living again. It was self-serving to do anything but that. Michael had suddenly been given permission to live and thrive, and he was filled with a new sense of purpose. His heart danced knowing that Violet was with him in the abstract sense. He rejoiced knowing that he could still make a difference in the world, that not all was lost, that he could achieve the things that he and Violet had spoken of many times. He was renewed. His loving, departed wife had reached through the veil and touched him. He knew it to be true. He would no longer spend his time in the numb existence in which he had kept himself since Violet passed, selfishly thinking of only himself when there was a whole world that he could help. Michael was born again.

"I knew these would be difficult assignments for you, Beautiful Soul. That is why I told you nothing of them before we came. You have proven yourself to be full of Grace and Divine presence. Your only assignment was to first give a touch of Angelic presence at the church and then to communicate with Michael through the light as he requested, but again you knew instinctively that you needed to take it a step further. You gave Michael the important message to move on with his life and not stay stagnant in the sorrow of the past. In doing this, you not only proved that the presence of Angels in a person's life is only a conversation away, but you allowed him the freedom to move forward so that he could make a difference in life, the difference that he was born to make."

"I am feeling very sad seeing him. I am not sure why I had to leave him, why was it that I had to leave him? We had a very good life together."

"It was your choice, Beautiful Soul. It was you who chose your purposes for that human life and when you would leave. Do you feel the truth in what I just reminded you of?"

"That is confusing to me; it does not make sense. If I was so happy and in love, then why would I choose to leave?"

"This is a good time for the next lesson, Beautiful Soul. Before each Golden Soul enters the human realm and unifies with a vessel of transportation in that realm, what they call a physical body, there are assignments given to, or rather chosen by, the soul. Each soul, before entering the human realm, makes decisions about what it is they will do, about the truths that they take to accomplish in their life- their Truth of Being and purposes. You see, Beautiful Soul; you made the decisions about what truths and purposes you would share and pursue prior to entering the human realm, just like all souls do. You made the choice to provide happiness and share love with all that you met in that life. You made the choice to share love and faith with your husband, Michael, in that life. You made the choice to help the lives of many humans in that life. Those things were your choices. How the life-line timing actually flows and how the events unfold is sometimes unknown, but the truths and purposes that each soul missions for themselves are woven into the make-up of the soul for that particular life. Your choices led you to an opportunity to not only help another's life, but to save a life and to attempt to save others. Very noble, Beautiful Soul."

"So you are saying that I went to that life knowing that I was going to lose my life in a fire? I knew I would leave my husband and family?"

"Beautiful Soul, often the exact events are not scripted for a life. There is no screenplay. Instead, souls entering the human realm will determine what truths they would like to accomplish, what purposes need to be addressed in that life at that time of existence to continue propelling them forward on their quest to Divine perfection. You went to that human life knowing that there were truths and purposes for you to accomplish, not how they would be accomplished, just that they had to be."

"So does each soul that enters the human realm with their own truths and purposes stay in the realm until the truths and purposes are realized?"

"Beautiful Soul, I will supply you an introductory teaching at this juncture. You will have a further lesson on this important condition when the time is right. First, yes, before they make the transition into the human realm, each soul entering the human realm chooses the things that it wants to achieve and address in each of its human lifetimes. Most transition into the realm through the human birthing process and join a human vessel in the infant stage, though some enter the human realm as walk-ins. The second part of the answer to your question is a difficult one and one that we here in this realm are working diligently to rectify. You see, Beautiful Soul; many of the Golden Souls that enter the human realm lose sight of their own truths and purposes and are unable to complete all the missions that they entered the life to achieve."

"I do not understand what you are saying. Why do they or would they lose sight of their own choices?"

"It is not done deliberately; these Golden Souls do not intentionally forget their own truths and purposes for the life they opted to enter. Instead, they have experienced transference off path; that is, they have been moved off their own path and onto the path of someone around them, perhaps the path of a parent, of another adult figure, or of other children. These other parties who disrupt the forward movement of another's individual purpose were themselves moved off their own paths and away from their truths of their being when they were just children, misplacing themselves, forgetting their truths and purposes, and losing sight of their distinct beckon that was to guide them through their own life. When these Golden Souls first enter the human realm, they know their truths, they recognize the reasons that they chose to enter the life; but sadly, they are deprogrammed off the path of self and onto the path of another. The older the child soul becomes, the more it forgets and by the age of eight, sometimes much younger depending on its life experiences to that point, it has completely forgotten its distinctive truth of being. It takes nearly a lifetime for these lost souls to remember why they entered their lives when they did. Sadly, some will never remember and will have to spend another human lifetime attempting to accomplish the same undertakings."

"How could what you are telling me be true? How could one forget the reason that one is living?"

"Let me ask you, Beautiful Soul, do you remember your truths and purposes for the life you just viewed, the one you lived with Michael?"

There was silence. The teacher allowed her time to completely call back the memories of that life.

"I do not remember any such things actually. I do not have many memories of my childhood. When I think about it, I become disheartened. Why is that? Why am I unable to remember the reason I am sad? "

"Beautiful Soul, do not wear the cloak of sorrow now for things that are finished and behind you. You are now learning a lesson that you can use to help from this point forward. I will explain why there is unhappiness in souls when they think back on these lost truths, on their lost purposes, even if they do not specifically remember what they were. Every soul feels incomplete and not whole when it lives off its path. It is as though something of importance is missing from its life. The reality is something of monumental importance *is* missing - the reason that it went to that particular life at that particular time. The problem that we need to correct is the redirecting of individual purpose and truths. As I mentioned, you will receive another lesson, but it is important to introduce you to this behavioral flaw because you now have learned and felt the effects of redirection of purpose in your recent human life. With this knowledge, you may begin opening yourself to the existence of redirection and then to the remedy.

"Though Earth Angels have many directives, one of the primary chosen missions is to help reverse this generations-old human pattern of desensitizing individual thinking and actions, of keeping humans off their own truths and independent thinking, and of streamlining thoughts to majority consensus. As you have been taught, supporting individual life missions is paramount including supporting divergent thinking as opposed to convergent thinking. Earth Angels are spreading the light of awareness about this through different channels of which you will learn more, but it is a slow wheel of evolution to turn."

"I have so many questions now, Teacher. I do not know what my purpose and truths were for this life I have just seen. What were they? You referred to it as my most recent human life; does that mean I had more human lives? What is an Earth Angel, that which you mention? Do we work in cooperation with them?"

"You have many questions, Beautiful Soul. Not a surprise. Firstly, yes, Beautiful Soul, you, like most souls, have lived many lives and many purposes and truths for each life. You will learn to open yourself up to the messages that you received along these lives. Patience as the memories appear to you like 'movies in your eyes.' Most souls live numerous and varied lives, each time entering a realm for predetermined purposes and truths, as we have spoken of. The goal is Mastery. Once Mastery has been accomplished, further missions are assigned based on the current needs in the galactic, the intergalactic, wherever a demand arises. The number of times that a soul elects to enter a human life is as varied as the number of assignments there are to accomplish and the efficiency with which the purposes are accomplished during a human life. If a soul is able to complete all the purposes in one human lifetime, then it moves on to the next mission that it needs to achieve in its progression to Mastery. However, if the soul is unable to accomplish all purposes, regardless the reason, then it will continue to reenter the human realm until the purposes are satisfied. As the soul completes its list of requirements to Mastery, sometimes more assignments are added. The current monumental shift that is underway is one such example. Many souls have been called into action to aid with this historically significant maneuver.

"You ask of Earth Angels. You have been provided an introduction to this lesson earlier. Briefly, Earth Angels are Angels that reenter the human realm and live a human life. Their purposes are of significant importance, are for the good of all realms, and are not focused on just their own advancements to Mastery because that has already been accomplished. During times of great change and expansions, Masters also enter a realm that is in need of assistance. For example, during the current progression on the earth, Earth Masters are living within the human realm. Just as Earth Angels have one foot in the human realm and one foot in the Angelic realm, so do Earth Masters have one foot in the human realm and one foot in the Master Realm. We are quite honored to work alongside these gurus.

"We will stay on task with the completion of our current lesson Now. You will learn to open yourself up to all the lessons that need to come to you when the assignment necessitates such. All will happen when the time for the information is essential. You cannot push something that is not ready to be moved. You cannot call on something that is not ready to participate and you cannot speak to someone who is not ready to listen. Remember, Beautiful Soul, have Faith in the process of your enlightenment, for you must receive and digest all the lessons for complete Mastery."

"Thank you teacher, I do have Faith. I will surround myself with the knowingness that my Faith will keep me aligned with the truths that are entwined in my being."

Chapter Five

The Lesson of Time for Universal Truths
of Now, Integration and Communication, and
The Age of "T's"

Time for Universal Truths of Now

"Remember, Beautiful Soul, there is no time here. Yesterday, today and tomorrow can all be seen through the same eye."

"I am confused with time, though. When I see the same human I saw before, it is different; time has changed it. That human has aged, but I am the same. How do I know how much time has passed between my assignments? When there is a new day?"

"You are thinking of time as it is in the human realm. That time does not exist here. We never age, we never grow old. We become wiser, more learned, but not visibly old as you witness in humans; and even in the human realm, the only thing that gets old is the vessel of operation and transportation, the body. Human souls advance, just as we do. So you see, Beautiful Soul, you do change, but not in the aged-vessel sense, the human-realm sense. You change in the expansion of knowledge you take in and through the advancement of shared knowledge that aid the universe."

"I know time is passing because I have new lessons and I have new assignments, but how do I know how much time has passed?"

"I do not understand why time is important to you. Why do you measure or use time like it is the marker for something? Time comes and time goes. Time was, is, and will be. That is all time is. It is not the measure of one's life here because if it were, the counting should have started hundreds, rather millions, of years ago. Time does not measure achievement, rather it limits one. If one judges all that is based on time, then one concentrates on a product that is not controllable. One must measure achievement on the sharing of Divine Truths for the purpose of mass enlightenment. Do not be concerned any longer with time as a measurement, Beautiful Soul.

"It is of great value to realize that sharing universal knowledge is advancement and that with every assignment and with every lesson we are creating opportunities for each soul and each realm to connect truths through the veils, to merge into the greatness of Divine consciousness of I Am. That is the valued measurement that warrants your attention; that warrants all soul's attention. To concentrate on the sharing of knowledge as it benefits universal higher consciousness is the key to advancement, not how much time has passed or will pass."

"I understand that which you speak of, Teacher. Then why is it we are hastened to help the human realm understand faster? Is that not a measure of time at its essence? Is it not time that we are concerned with when we help the human realm integrate the lessons more rapidly?"

"You are wise, Beautiful Soul. Understand this: when humans integrate a lesson expeditiously, then they have not only raised their awareness, they have raised the awareness of every human's consciousness that they come into contact with. The more humans we aid in immediate integration, the higher the sum of consciousness via their radius of influence. If we were to concentrate on the time for such achievements, we would have a limited measuring stick based on the human's vessel of existence, rather than the soul's continuous existence. The human vessel is limited, and based on a human timeline, however, the soul lives on limitlessly, sharing and spreading truths and knowledge from all times and all places. Our concentration must be on the sharing of information and not on the time that it takes to do so. The more we share, the higher the universal vibration will become."

"I understand teacher. Expeditious sharing of knowledge; creates mass advancements which create amplified universal wisdom."

"Everything that has happened in the past is the Now of today. It is the Now that we can affect. We cannot affect the past, just the Now—just this Now to set in motion the Now of the future."

Human Integration and Communication

"We give humans communications for their advancement in many ways: during their recharging period, meaning through their dreams in their sleeping hours; during their meditative period of focused meditation or daydreaming; and during their waking periods. The lessons and messages that we give to humans may take a period to integrate into their being. The lesson, the intensity of the transmissions, the scope of utilization, and the level of acceptance by the human all determine the time it takes for the lesson to be fully assimilated. When a human is aware enough to give intention to the lessons and messages they receive, the integration happens more rapidly."

"Your energy feels different to me, different than the other teachers I have had."

"You are correct in your assessment. I am from a different realm. You are familiar with the vibration of the Angelic realm, the gentle energy of the Angelic realm. I am from the Masters realm for lack of a better qualifier. All the realms work closely together to aid in this massive enlightenment project."

"So you are a Master? There was talk of the Master Realm and the Masters in a different lesson. I am not familiar with other realms? Will I learn more about them?"

"Heaven is more expansive than most know. We will teach you of more realms in a different lesson. There are many realms and we all cooperate and coordinate our efforts for universal progression. This current shift in collective evolution is one of the largest that has been endeavored to this point in Now. Each realm is sharing the genius knowledge that is its Mastery to streamline the measures necessary for complete efficiency. You will learn from many, not just the Angelic realm, but from all realms, for it will take all realms in a united front to orchestrate the shift that is required Now. It is important to understand this, that All of All is coordinating an advancement unparalleled to that which has been attempted or achieved before. The human realm must be enlightened by this collective effort to reach the end result of this huge collaborative effort. Many humans keep themselves behind a mask that creates an illusion of reality. They see themselves as very little, instead of as the magnificence that they are. It is as though their

Page 113

vision of themselves is a mirror without reflection. They can only see void and darkness. They strain to see but are summoned by the void. Help is all around them—The Earth realm, the Nature realm, the Aquatic realm—but they do not see these realms as an aid to them. They do not see these realms as a participating factor in the greatness of I Am. Instead, they ignore the vibration of these realms, even though they are or can be visible to them.

The challenge of having these desensitized humans see and sense realms such as the Angelic, Master, Fairy, and Celestial realms that are not immediately visible to them, is requiring a convergent effort of awareness. When humans do not physically see the realms and the importance of realms visible and invisible, there is no sense of respect, support, or belonging; and it becomes an even larger, though imperative, task for us to enlighten this human realm—the entire human realm—masses and masses at a time. When we shine our lights on humans' images so that humans can see themselves in the mirror, so they can see their souls' image clearly, then their awareness of all that is and can be expands to a magnificent radius. Their up-to-date view of themselves as greatness, this newly recognized image of themselves, then touches other humans who require the lesson. These recently enlightened humans can help shine their light in the mirrors of the humans who have lost sight of their Divine image. When humans are able to see themselves again for the splendor of their being, then they are able to open all their senses to the Mastery of the universal Divine. In doing so, they begin to see, for the first time, the importance of all the realms— the Nature, Earth, Aquatic and Fairies realms- not just those that they can immediately see and they gain Faith in the knowledge of expanded realms. They will begin trusting in the realms that are not immediately visible and trusting in the expansion of knowledge, expansion of truths, and thus in the expansion of All that is and will be.

Let us talk now about the human intention of message integration now."

"What do you mean by intention, Master?"

"When humans are consciously aware, they will understand that some of the dreams they have, some of the daydreams, and even waking experiences they encounter, are messages and lessons sent to them by Divine Grace. These humans then receive the lessons and messages readily and integrate them with intention, by thinking and saying to themselves or aloud something like, " Thank you for the messages and lessons that you have gifted me. I receive them fully and with Faith that everything sent to me from Divine is for my highest and best use."

Humans who show appreciation and indicate that they recognize and value the lessons and messages as sacred and Divinely blessed will amalgamate and assimilate the messages that we send them more quickly and will be ready for further lessons sooner. The more humans learn to integrate gifts quickly, the higher the vibration on earth will become and the more quickly universal consciousness will be raised. Therefore, it is our job to also teach those in the human realm the importance of assimilation of Divine gifts into their very being."

"Master, how are we to teach the human realm this lesson?"

By Thinking,
So it is,
By Speaking,
So it is,
By Acting,
So it is.

"Yes, I understand this basic law of like equals like, of doing equals results. Please help me to understand how we may help the human realm understand things that are out of their logical vision and scope. It seems most humans operate with little Faith in their own abilities and their own inner guidance. It is as though they have shut down the ability to listen to the sacred truths and gifts that they took with them to their current life. Instead, they doubt their own proficiencies and base their decisions on those of others through logical presentation. They have forgotten that the soul houses all the truths of ancient wisdom and that they must tap into that knowledge to advance in their current life. How Master may we help humans to see within, without doubt, for the answers they seek? How may we help humans remember the path that they chose for themselves prior to entering their current life? How Master, may we help the human realm feel with Faith that the messages they receive are actual gifts from Divine and that they must act upon them and integrate them into their being?"

"The questions you ask are broad, but parallel. Let me first correct you; nothing is out of the human-realm scope if it is provided to them by Divine. Everything given to the human realm is in balance with all that is and should

Page 117

be. You are correct in respect to unfilled purpose paths, the desensitizing of individuals to soul's truths, and the human realm's inability to recognize and have Faith in their own internal knowingness. It is with much earnestness that we choose to address the shadows of doubt and fear that have enveloped the human realm and that are creating weakness and suffering instead of pure light and advancement at a pace that is Divinely possible. For universal solvency we must aid all realms in their advancement.

"You are assigned to the human realm at this time. You seek answers to your questions of how we may provide aid to the human realm, help it hear our messages more clearly, and help it understand that what it is hearing is true and real and Divinely sent. That is what you are asking, is it not? How may we aid the human realm in a belief bigger than itself, aid humans to adopt a belief in greatness beyond limit in a free-flowing pact through all veils? We may help the human realm with everything—with knowledge and with the sharing and integration of universal wisdom administered with pure love and Divine intention. How, you ask, are we to share this knowledge with a realm that is unaware or un-accepting of things they do not see or think possible? This has been a true debate and enigma throughout realms and throughout history. How do we help those who are not aware they need help? How do we help those who are not asking because they do not know better or know to ask? How do we help those who refuse to see there is anything better beyond their immediate vision of reality? The questions you ask are not new ones. They are questions that we have battled with throughout the ages, generations, and seasons.

"It is Now that we will, without exception, take stances to move from the deliberating to the doing. We will take greater measures to ensure the human realm feels the messages that we give it are truth and are sent with pure love for the betterment of all kind. We will help the human realm see and feel by sending prophets in the form of individual messengers to the masses of humans. We will stay with the humans until they feel that there is truth to what they have received. We will continue to send messages via the messengers until the consciousness of humans, one by one, then hundreds by hundreds, then thousands by thousands, shifts the level of belief to one of pure Divine knowingness, shifts the intensity of belief to levels the universe has never seen, all by empowering each human with truths that will magnify thought consciousness and by empowering each human to see the beauty of their own Divine reflection. We will have not one prophet working hard to pass along the information; we will have many messengers spreading the word of Divine.

"How, you ask, are we able to accomplish this now, when it has not been accomplished before, when the whole of all mankind has done nothing but falter and fall?

"I ask you, are we not Divine and, therefore is not everything possible with Divine?

"You ask why then has Divine not stepped in to achieve these feats before now?

"And, now you ask, how do these many messengers help the human realm to hear and believe that they have a duty to help universal awareness?

"The answer is as vast and as simple as this: we Now have Faith above Faith.

That is the energy that we are sending with pure love everywhere and that is the energy that is being readily received- Faith above Faith."

Telepathic Communication

"Beautiful Soul, I have returned to you for this lesson. You will have two teachers on this important subject I will stay with you and begin your teaching and then you will experience a new teacher. We have both been assigned to this teaching because two realms wish to be represented in this presentation.

This is a vested project of the universe; but because of its degree of challenges, including its requiring active human involvement, the lesson will be much more difficult to infuse into the human realm. As you know, free will allows humans the ability to make their own choices, even those that we see as harmful to them and others. We can instruct and aid, but there is a limit to our involvement.

"Thank you, Teacher. I look forward to learning more with you. You mentioned that two realms wish involvement. Which other realm will be joining us?"

"We are honored to have another representative of the Master Realm with us. In many realms communication is channeled telepathically. Such is the case in these Angelic and Master realms. We read one another's thoughts, feel one another's feelings, and sense who they are and when they are with us. You have learned this in some degree already. The human realm has yet to realize this ability. When their realm elevates to the realization of this ability, it will induce any reluctant participants to think more kindly and act in a more Divine way. You see, some humans think badly of others and carry bad feelings and thoughts; however, they present themselves in a different manner. Their words do not represent their thinking.

"When the human realm is infused with telepathic communication, those humans will no longer be able to hide in falsehood. They will be known for what they think and feel. Realms that communicate telepathically maintain good thoughts and actions.

"Humans may practice this shift to kinder thoughts at first because they will be revealed and visible to others, but they will continue the practice because they will recognize the tremendous advantages of positive thinking over the weight and effects of negative thinking.

Maintain Good Thoughts

and

Speak and Act the same

Now

For Every Action, there is a Reaction.

Whether at the realization of telepathy or not maintain good thoughts and actions."

She felt then a shift and swirling vibration in the energies around her. This energy felt heavier than the Angelic Teacher vibrations she was accustomed to.

"Teacher, what is this new vibration I sense?"

"Beautiful Soul, you have perceived your Master teacher's presence."

"Soul, listen, for what I teach is crystalline of value," spoke the Master.

The Age of "T's" is Nearing

"Telepathy, Transporting, and Transparency to name a few—Earth Angels are tasked with assimilating this value and implication. The Angelic realm and the Master realm as well as other realms aid with the transmission of this dispatch. It is a universal alliance assigned by Source in sense, to create recognition, develop illumination, and administer functionality. Transparency is the focal integration in this Now and will maintain supreme position until such time as rank changes.

"Thoughts, words, and actions must align because it will be most evident who is speaking or acting with truth and who is still hiding truths. Because of transparency, one's thoughts and actions will create full disclosure of one's soul. Those who speak in patterns that do not bring into alignment the thoughts that are contained within them, who speak in words that are sent from their voices that do not mirror the actions that they take, will become clear examples of conflict. Because of transparency, it will be evident those who are parallel with truth and those who continue to create a facade.

As it stands in this Now, many humans think poorly of other humans, degrade other humans in their minds, and perhaps even speak these degrading words to a third party in an effort to unify, creating a negative environment. This negative environment mingles with all other atmospheres. Then these same humans take actions and speak words to the humans they have just mentally belittled or have spoken poorly of behind their backs—actions or words that are in direct conflict with their thinking. They wear two faces, a face they show to others and a face they keep to themselves and a few chosen others. They think with vinegar, speak with honey.

The Age of Transparency will no longer afford these divided humans an opportunity to hide behind a sheath. Thoughts will be as clearly understood as the spoken word is now. Actions will be felt and will be visible; thoughts will be felt and will be visible. Humans will no longer be able to speak poorly of others and have those negative thoughts hidden. This will be difficult for many humans who maintain a pattern of speaking words that are not in alignment with their thoughts.

"The Universal Consciousness is vastly gratified for this new move to transparency of character in all realms; for, in design, it will allow those who are virtuous in their patterns to continue expanding at a faster pace and it will prompt those less virtuous to become aware of maintaining higher quality thoughts and actions. As I have taught, beings will no longer be able to hide from their discrepancies. At first, some will implement more congruent action and thought from a place of fear that their actual thoughts and actions will be discovered. But because every soul is of Divine design and knows the brilliance of feeling the magnificence of such, humans will begin practicing an alliance of good thoughts, actions, and words for its own sake. This practice will continue to lighten them and, in turn, will lighten those around them; the domino effect will result, one light shining on another, which will shine on another, and so forth. Do you understand that which I instruct you on, for your understanding of this is category to development?"

"Yes, Master, I understand that which you speak of and teach. I too was saddened to observe the balancing act that many humans exercise. Speaking in one direction with the winds of their firebomb words, yet moments later, turning in a different direction with different words, enveloping themselves in conflict due to their own words, thoughts and actions."

"There is a large positive directive accompanying the transparency of humans. The shift to transparency will be a contributing factor in preventing events of the past from transpiring again, events such as Atlantis when the lower energies hid behind masks of good, coaxing humans to them only to take over and rule with black, negatively charged intentions, controlling from a place of false realness, as has been spoken of before. Each human soul's truths will shine through for all to see and; because of this, the lower energies and negative energies will no longer be able to hide behind a false veil to gain control. This blackness of duplicity, which has cursed civilizations for centuries, will no longer find space in a realm whose visibility is transparent. Unable to find adequate housing and being outnumbered by the new, advanced, higher frequency communications being ignited throughout the human realm in percentages never witnessed before, the lower energies and negative energies will be unable to exist and will therefore dissipate into dust to be recharged into Divine light.

" Mother Earth has had her Drudges in center earth protecting her crystals from the immorality of these black energies of which I speak. The Drudges have closely encircled the crystals, encasing them with their protection, hiding them. Now, because of the shifting to higher consciousness, Mother Earth will finally be able to have the Drudges back away and thus open up the crystals and allow their radiance to sparkle and charge all the crystals throughout the world and universe. There are many affirmative reactions that will occur as this shift continues, the likes of which we have not observed before. Do you understand the magnitude of this component in the equation? "

"Yes, Master, it is of imperative nature that these lower and negative energies fall off into nothingness, to be reformed into light, for the brilliance of Divine and the betterment of the universe. There will be no space for those wishing to hide behind a reflection that is not theirs. Progress from this will be unchartered and unequaled."

"You have received this lesson well. Begin Now with this practice."

Chapter Six

The Lesson of Earth Angels
And
Wounded Human Position

"There was mention that I would receive further information about the Earth Angels, about what Teacher said I was in the human realm. May I have more of this lesson now, please."

"Hello, New One. I will give you this lesson on human Angels, known as Earth Angels."

"Thank you, Teacher, you have energy that I have not felt before. Thank you for sharing your knowledge with me. Why do you call me" New One"? It feels as if I have been in this Now for a lengthy time."

"All souls that join the Angelic realm to perform Angelic missions are considered new until they are released to perform assignments on their own. Until that day you and all new studies will, in theory, be new. And, yes, I am new to you. Just as it is in other realms, some guides are more gifted at communication on a particular subject matter than others. This is my area, and I will share with you what you have to learn. You ask about Earth Angels as though you have forgotten your role in your past life. Is that the case, New One?"

"Yes, Teacher, I am still calling forward all the memories of what was to my Now. I was unaware that I was an Earth Angel until my last teacher advised me of it. I can remember having felt different in my past life as though I did not fit in completely with everything and everyone around me, but that is all that has entered my thinking consciousness at this time. May I ask, Teacher, who releases me to perform assignments on my own?"

"Your truths will continue to integrate to enlighten you. Allow the process the time it requires. There is a sector within our realm, a department, which monitors advancements. You will learn more of the Angelic departments, agreements and cooperation through further lessons. Let us focus on your question of Earth Angels, that which brought me to you. You were told of the existence of Earth Angels when you first joined us, do you recall?"

"Yes, Teacher, I do remember that lesson. I seek further knowledge now, if you please."

"Earth Angels are both human and Angelic. Earth Angels balance the human life with the Divine path they have come to lead. Despite the reactions of others to them, they forge forward knowing that pure Divine is within everyone. They nurture and celebrate the knowingness of this truth. It is a difficult path for them in many cases because the darkness reacts to their good and sends to them people who have allowed the darkness to engulf them. These souls challenge the Earth Angels with belittling words and actions, demeaning them and their choices, sending them psychic stabbings and negative energy, making every attempt possible to keep them from generating and spreading the goodness of Divine Light, and bullying them into submission by peer pressure and threats of being different, weird, or out of touch with reality.

Earth Angels struggle a great deal based on their grounding in the human realm until they learn to open their consciousness to allow transmission of communication from the Angelic realm. The threads of Angelic truths woven into their beings provide them the unspoken inner sense of how things should be, the right and Divine path of the Angelic realm. But the humans around them, who are not operating at the higher and advanced consciousness level, shut down these Earth Angels' consciousness and influence them to operate in lower levels of consciousness.

"The fear of advancement into something that cannot be physically monitored is the human side of Earth Angels, creating a true conflict within. The shift to higher consciousness that is underway Now will aid these Earth Angels greatly."

"Do Earth Angels know who they are? Do they at some point realize that they are not like other humans and are tasked with more?"

"Look inside yourself for the answers, New One; remember you have all that you need."

"As you say, Teacher, I will do."

"Earth Angels deal with disappointment more than humans and are unsure of why until this higher level of communiqué and bond is honored. Once connected, their Divine sense of purpose is ignited and they are charged with purpose beyond their initial understandings. Sadly, some Earth Angels have been covered with such heavy cloaks of self-sacrifice and self-belittlement and a sense of insignificance and worthlessness that they are unable to clearly make this Divine connection. Some, forgetting that pure love and Faith conquer all and build bridges to the pathways of their Truth of Being, allow just a small stream of the joyous abundance of Divine light to radiate to them, only a hint of what is truth. Then they quickly shut it off, gathering the perceived safety of their cloak around them in fear that they will get their hopes up to fall yet again. Not realizing the strongest protection is Faith.

Faith through storms,
Faith through doubts,
Faith through struggles,

Page 135

Faith above Faith.

"They witness in threads the human realm, humans taking paths and making decisions that are less than the Divine way of truths that is woven within them. They become saddened, hurt, and disappointed by such actions but unsure why they have such deep reactions when others around them do not. Since their complete memories of Divine perfection and the Angelic realm become blurred when they are involved in human life, they struggle with understanding and forgiveness, especially when someone around them they care for betrays them and take actions that are improper, immoral, or self-degrading- actions less than the perfection that they inherently know exists. Earth Angels have a strong sense of right and wrong and that sense is challenged greatly in the human realm. Their human side is tempted to become judgmental because they have the sense of what is correct Divine perfection, yet the Angelic side struggles with the imperfection of judgment.

We are profoundly committed to helping the Earth Angels sort out these imbalances and to helping them protect their hearts and souls from the pain of witnessing the indiscretions and trespasses committed by some humans. Lessons have to be taught and learned, but it is our intention that they are done without our constituent being damaged. We teach them not to take the actions of others personally.

The lessons are given as teachings for them and other humans, not to harm and hinder but to enlighten for advancement. Unfortunately, because of the separation from knowledge that occurs once the Angel enters the human realm as an Earth Angel and because the human realm has, until the current realignments, been operating in the third dimension, much of the information that we teach is in a place that cannot be accessed without higher conscious levels, which take time for many Earth Angels to remember and re-access."

"You speak of third-dimension thinking. Is that the level at which all humans register?"

"Though it is changing in the sense that many humans are allowing the fog of containment to move from them and they are accepting the unlimited possibilities of what can be, many humans remain in the cemented customs, limits, and beliefs of past, thus the third dimension. Humans are opening to the new messages and tones that are being shared by our appointed messengers and because of this they are rising in vibration. There is a streamline effect taking place that is elevating the human realm to the fifth dimension. Whether all humans are aware of this or not, all who remain at this time in the human realm are participating. Some humans may choose to drop off and return to the human realm at a time when things are not in such a large transition. Transitions are change and often cause unexplained actions. Some actions are chaotic and too difficult to manage. Changes of this magnitude take time. It is not immediate and there are several shifts that take place, some felt and some not felt.

The Earth Angels, Earth Masters, and our messengers are sharing vibrations of the seventh dimensional thinking and processing with those they feel are prepared and ready. Messiahs, Prophets and Guides operate in this seventh dimension now. Some operate in the eleventh dimension, but that tone is not readily recognized by most. The lay lines and grids surrounding the earth have been placed. The appointed guides for the grids are stationed. These structures aid in the fluid transformation as best as can be. This is the biggest undertaking that has ever been asked of the unified front of realms. It is taking complete integration of all realms' intentions to trigger a shift in dimensional thinking such as that which is happening in the human realm. It is time that the humans take their place as leaders and menders in the cosmic conglomerate of progression. The human realm for too long has required attention and aid. It is time for it to take its place in developing and improving universal functions for evolution and participate in support to other realms for their advancements.

Let us return to the original lesson of Earth Angels now. That which you asked of initially New One. Not all lessons are given to the Earth Angels to teach; some lessons come from humans. Interestingly, in these cases, not all the humans are prepared to learn the lesson they are teaching in this lifetime. Some are sent to create an opportunity for others to learn, but they themselves remain oblivious to both. That fact confuses Earth Angels, too, until they come to realize it. You see, as stated before, the hardest thing we have to face is the fact that, when Earth Angels enter the human realm, they enter as humans so their memory of this Angelic realm registers at a higher vibration than is easily accessible in the human realm. The Angelic realm and many other realms register at higher vibrations than are readily intercepted by lower vibration realms. These higher vibrations are accessible, but that is a learned thing and most humans do not realize that they can achieve it. Even Earth Angels do not know that they are Earth Angels in many cases. They do not know that they are in fact living a life of both an Angel and a human at the same time. They do not understand that the reason they have such difficulty accepting the harsh actions of some humans is because they have experienced Divine and are part of Divine to help shine Divine light on humans. Some Earth Angels will achieve these realizations in their human lifetime and that will aid them with their dealings; some will not. To help Earth Angels and save them from such sadness—that is something that we are dedicated to repair."

"Is there not a way that we can inform the Earth Angels of their value to the universe by supplying them the needed information upon arrival in the human realm? It seems that copious time would be saved with the discovery and considerably more would be accomplished as a result."

"You are wise for recognizing the importance of the component. As I stated, it is an element we are addressing. If more humans believed in and practiced instantaneous manifestation, this task and conversation would be unnecessary at this juncture. We cannot push humans to do more than they are aware they are capable of doing at the time, even though we see the potential they possess. Because of free will, ultimately all final decisions lie with the human. We must recognize, but not interfere with, the decisions they make, even though it is difficult for us to back away sometimes. This is especially true when a human is so close to discovery, so close to the end of a long-awaited mission that will line up their next paths of purpose and truths. That is where we are lucky to be gifted with the Divine skill of Faith and patience, knowing that All will be, perhaps not in the time frame that we see possible, but it will be. Humans have the desire but lack the wherewithal for different reasons, including resistance. It is this resistance they maintain that we must help them see and then help them clear."

"Yes teacher, I feel sadness and loss for the humans when I see what I can see, what we all can see; and I realize that many come so close but then give up, faltering just before completion. If only we could gift them with a quick vision of what we see."

"They have the ability to engage their own vision; and we are working on the transparency aspect, as you have been taught. As stated Earth Angles learn lessons at the same time as they are teaching them. This gets confusing for them because they feel they need to give the lessons; however, the human side of them needs to learn lessons too. Often the confrontations and problems they encounter in their human life are the lessons they must learn from and then teach others. Sadly some stay within the confrontations and do not lift themselves out from the darkness and chaos to a level of higher knowing.

There is so much we wish Earth Angels would remember when they enter the human realm instead of having to relearn the knowledge during their lifetimes. Just like the bulk of the human realm, they have to relearn the missions that they carried to their current life to accomplish because of having been taken off their path by other humans who had strayed as well.

Earth Angels possess abilities far beyond those they recognize they have because they have forgotten their Angelic teachings, as I have taught you. Earth Angels have the ability to create harmony in everything around them. They know harmony. They have lived harmony in the Angelic realm and they have witnessed harmony in other realms; they have simply forgotten. There are so many intentional distractions in the human realm to keep humans from the truths of Divine. Lower energies running rampant. If every Earth Angel were to practice the tool of creating complete harmony around themselves in not only the human realm but also in the Fairies, Nature, Aquatic, and Earth, realms, it would be an incredible neutralizer of all the physical, mental and spiritual toxins that enter the realms and then become so entrenched.

"What do you mean harmony in everything around them? What are these *other realms* to which you refer? What other abilities do humans have that they do not know they have?"

"Slow yourself, New One, slow yourself. We are on the lesson of Earth Angels, we shall remain with this subject until it is deemed time that we are not."

"Yes, Teacher, I understand and I apologize. I feel I have much to learn and perhaps at times I want to take all the lessons in at the same time."

"A worthy trait, eagerness to accept more as the student so that you may become a better teacher. The best teachers are those who continue to grow as students. Remember this, one who is attempting to catch many fish with one dip of the hand, may lose them all; however, one who dips his hand in an attempt to catch just one fish has given full attention to that task and, thus, may be rewarded with many."

"I will give full attention to this lesson, Teacher, I understand. Thank you for helping me envision the clarity."

"Earth Angels need to balance time spent between realms. The more they open and raise their consciousness to what is, the more they recognize and appreciate the sense of unconditional Divine love in the Angelic realm. The radiance of Oneness infuses them and they want to spend more time with it. As humans, they tend to daydream and to be spacey, flighty, distracted, forgetful, and sometimes inattentive during conversations. They may seem to have changed and to have become detached, distant, and uninvolved in human-life activity. The more time spent in the Angelic realm, the less effective they are in the human realm.

Of course, Earth Angels do need to tend to the business they have in the Angelic realm, opening themselves to the messages and lessons they are to share and teach, opening their consciousness for full effectiveness. At the same time, they must remember their assignments for the human life and remember to strive for the discipline required to balance the two realms. Our department for monitoring Earth Angel activities aids in this balancing, pulling them back to the balance of both realms, reminding them of their all important roles in each. Some Earth Angels are sensitive to our involvement and make necessary adjustments and some are not. Yet another measure we are working on."

"I can understand, Teacher, why some Earth Angels would want to spend more of their energetic time in the Angelic realm. Some of the human realm energies are dark and angry, exceptionally difficult to be near, though there are humans whom I have encountered who are tremendously giving and caring. We are all working together to spread more of this positive energy. I see and feel this now, Teacher. Lighter energy floats, heavier energy sinks."

"Accurate, New One. We send Earth Angels to different kinds of lives, spreading them out to share their all-important services in the human realm. No matter what life they lead, they have one thing in common: spreading Divine light, as you say, spreading the positive energy. The more light that shines throughout all that is, the harder time negative energies have in holding their position and they eventually dissipate into nothingness to be reabsorbed and rebuilt into Divine light. One light illuminates a path, two lights a road, and so forth."

"I have further questions, would you be so kind as to help me with the answers?"

"I have no guarantee that the answers I have for you will suffice, although I sense that the lesson that you wish to have now will be important. Please ask it of me and we will determine whether this is something that I assist you with or you will have an alternative teacher for the lesson, New One."

"Teacher, do Earth Angels become full Angels after their human assignment? Are they more advanced than humans? Do they always remain an Earth Angel?"

"I had a sense that the questions I received from you, New One, would warrant attention and tempo far greater than the average query. You have not proven that sense wrong. The questions you ask are not easy ones to answer because they have multiple answers, just as there are multiple Earth Angels. I will stay with you for this question, but we may be Graced with the wisdom from another as well. Every soul grows with each experience, whether that experience is of negative pursuit or positive pursuit. The ultimate goal is to be of pure Divine creation, so that the soul radiates with nothing short of Divine perfection. It is with this attainment that graduation is realized. Achieving this highest pedestal in the Divine order of things requires devotion and affirmation.

"To instruct you, Earth Angels are already Angels; they have just elected to join the human realm at a time when more assistance is required. Their purposes for joining the human realm are of advanced nature; but since all souls contribute to the completion of Oneness, they work concurrently with souls that have not yet achieved Mastery level. The Earth Angel's soul may elect to live continuous lives in the human realm if it deems the need for doing so based on the current status of affairs or accomplishments that are slated for achievement. Or, the Earth Angel may live only one life as an Earth Angel in the human realm. As taught before, since they are of Angelic design, their full intention is for the betterment of all to reach Divine level of I Am and Oneness. Therefore, they will volunteer service to this end in as many realms as seen fit. As is witnessed throughout time, many of the major advancements have been when someone from a Mastery realm, such as an Angel enters the human realm as a human. Human life is for a specified period of time for a specified reason. The soul lives on; it is simply the human vessel that wears out. Divine life is completeness and Oneness of everything."

"Why teacher do humans- let me rephrase- many humans keep themselves in such depths of sadness and unknowing? Why do they not reach higher to gain fulfillment and happiness? Since they are part of Divine, a portion of them must yearn for the pure acceptance, beauty, and love of the Oneness of which they are."

"Hello, Beautiful Soul, I have been asked to help you with is lesson."

"Welcome, Teacher, I am happy to be with you."

"We have supplied you an introduction to a portion of this lesson in a prior teaching and now I will further this session. There are a multitude of answers to your one question and a variety of reasons for humans not consciously seeking Divine, most of which involve the complete unawareness by the humans of their actions and effects of their actions. At this juncture, I will teach you three reasons.

The first and admittedly the saddest for most of us is the fact that there are humans that do not believe in us; they do not believe in Angels. There are even some humans that do not believe in God, Creator, Higher Being, Source, whatever the chosen name. If they do not believe in us, then they do not know they have help from a place beyond the immediate visible plane. They lack the wherewithal to seek answers due to their lack of belief. Though it brings us a sense of joyous relief to report the number of disbelievers is dropping, it still saddens us that any exist at all. One cause of the lack of belief has been displays of lower energy involvement in the human realm, which creates such explosively devastating scenes, such horrific acts, that they can only be credited to involvement of lower negative energies. It takes much work to gather this darkness together and dispel it from further involvement. These instances drag belief down, but belief then rebounds up at a level higher than where it was before the negative events.

We are dedicated to expanding our light so that we may shine it more fervently on those in need and then taking the next step, helping them shine their light with more intensity on others, who in turn will do the same. Light over dark. We are dedicated to opening up passageways that have been locked due to the disappointments of vast ages that were entrapped by darkness leaching itself through what good dared remain. We are dedicated to demonstrating that it is safe to trust and have Faith in something that is bigger than human eyes can see, to facilitating the full utilization of souls' senses so that they can feel Divine presence, and to showing ourselves to humans in ways that their analyzing minds will receive. When humans know of our existence, know that we are here to help them and wish to help them, then sadness will be replaced with joyous possibilities of what can be and true visualization of what is.

"The next important reason for sorrow and despondency within the human populous is that many humans are living a life that is not theirs, as you have been schooled of before. They are attempting to operate using another human's controls, as though they are driving their vessel remotely from another person's vessel or allowing someone else to drive their craft. Humans, as we have discussed before, are souls that have elected to enter the human realm, either for the first time or again. They make a conscious choice about what their truth of being and their purposes will be based on their own desires for fulfillment, which are also aligned with the universal matrix. When they enter the human realm, much of their inbred purpose for being there is taught out of them."

"Taught out of them, Teacher?"

"Yes, Beautiful Soul, this is nothing new; it has happened for more time than is readily available. There is a pattern of moving the beautiful Golden Souls, children that are born, off their own purpose path, away from their own truths of being, and onto a path that is comfortable for the adults around them, whether that is by the Golden Soul's parents, relatives, or peers. Slowly the mission-charged soul is steered away from the reason it entered its life at a particular time. This redirecting is done by humans who, in fact, were redirected the same way, away from their own truths and purposes and forced to think, walk, and learn again, this time according to someone else's rules. This pattern of convergent thinking is usually intensified as the children attend their educational facilities. Teachers program desired behavior out of necessity, not intention. There is no ill intent. It is what it is until it is something different. We are charged with sharing this message, making it an integral part of human realm thinking: each Golden Soul, each child who enters life, must be supported so that each may share the Divine reasons for which they entered

Page 151

their life at a particular time. We are spreading enlightening values to the humans who live now: that every soul is different and every soul is sent for a specific reason. Whatever the case, every human should be recognized for the important roles that he or she has been sent to play. Children need to be supported to follow the path that they are inherently drawn to."

"What you speak of, Teacher, is of powerful concern. I feel the passion of this lesson. Though the human sight has been limited by its own failure to exercise expanded vision, I would assume if humans were able to comprehend the magnitude of progression that could be created in the universe, if each human were to follow his or her purpose and truths of being, they would be much more prone to individual

purpose support.

"As it relates to the sadness in the human realm, I understand the inner frustrations souls must feel when they are charged with particular missions for their lives but are unable to accomplish them because they are driving in another's lane. Is that all the reasons that humans do not seek help, Teacher? They do not believe in us and they cannot remember the reasons for their human life?"

"It is not all; you will learn one more reason as this lesson progresses, but this teaching has not ended.

"You are correct, Beautiful Soul, in that it creates immeasurable amounts of sorrow when souls are unable to perform the duties that they themselves chose to address. This is especially true when they are aware they made choices before entering their human forms, are aware of the impact their chosen missions could have on the universe, and are falling short of the magnificence they anticipated. Humans who have been taken off their path, the path that was blessed by Divine, live a life that does not satisfy them. They are not filled with the joys experienced by those who operate in the truths for their being. Instead they feel unproductive, they do not like their jobs; some do not even like their lives. There is a sense of sadness that brews within them, a sadness attributed to unfulfilled purposes.

"Not all humans live out of alignment with their truths and purposes; not all humans are taken off their track when the soul enters the human realm, but sadly many are. If you remember, your previous lesson taught you that we are sending aid to the human realm. We step in when humans have fallen off their path and something will or has happened to prevent them from naturally realigning with it .

"So that the matrix of events maintains its correct stability and direction, we monitor the human realm. There are Angels here, a special task force, have you, entitled the Monitoring Angels, whose job it is to monitor purpose progress, applying the progress made to the universal grid of advancement. When they identify a transgression in purpose that will not automatically correct itself to align back to truth, then that section notifies us and we step in to aid the human and prevent an unscheduled loss.

"As has been shared before, keeping souls on track with their own truths of being and purposes is our biggest agenda. The Earth Angels are on task for helping with this, Beautiful Soul. There are souls on earth that we step in and help. We enter their lives and create experiences that deliberately knock them off the erroneous path that they are on in hopes that the repositioning will trigger the memory of who they really are and why they are living the life they are living. In time, you will observe examples of this. We may even receive an assignment to help a human with this repositioning. These are difficult assignments because we must inflict pain of sorts to aid the soul in remembering."

"So what you are saying, Teacher, is that we create situations for a soul, a human soul, that are difficult for it, just so that it will remove itself from the distractions it has been keeping itself in and, as such; be able to realign with itself with the reasons why it is present in its life? Do all humans understand that our creating difficulty is for the better good? Do all humans realign themselves with their truth after such experiences?"

"Beautiful Soul, please understand, we do not harm for harm's sake; we aid in the realignment of a soul's chosen purpose and truths. In some instances, that requires us to create situations for humans that allow them the opportunity to think beyond their immediate scope. Sometimes humans become so obsessed with a situation they cannot see the whole of the situation. They begin thinking too much and create chaos over something that should deserve no further attention. In doing so they take time away from things that they themselves want to do in their lifetime. A simple solvable problem, such as a disagreement with another human, takes on an all-consuming role in the human's life and drains them, siphoning off time and energy that should be used on the betterment of things designed for all mankind. It is in situations like these that we step in and give nudges in different ways. We have some highly charged souls in the human realm now who have chosen to make universal differences in their lives. They too get distracted by the fog of illusion, lower energies, and negative energies because, of course, they are human. Before they entered their human lives, these souls knew of the potential distractions that plague humans and asked that we help them stay on track with their purpose, no matter how and how many times. These souls want to stay true to their truths.

"Just as one thread woven over and over into itself can make something of beauty to be worn and admired, so too is it that the human soul's missions can weave in and out to create greatness far outreaching the span of sight and immediate thought. By aiding souls with the visions of their Divinely blessed desires, we are aiding the woven canopy of universal advancements. One soul's purpose plays into another soul's purpose, which plays into another's, all weaving the advancements. Some of the most beautiful garments are woven with threads that are of varied textures and colors. This is similar to the human souls involved. Each human soul has a mission, not like another's, but equally important to the durability of the finished product.

Some souls' contributions may seem of little value compared to other souls' involvement; but without all souls' threads working together supporting one another, the project would be incomplete or not as magnificent as it could be with continuity, alliance, and group support and participation.

"You have much more to learn and you have learned much. All will come to you when you need it. Just remember that with the help of God, Divine Creator, we can help all that are to be helped. I am here to cover the standard practices with you. The style of help will be given to you when you most need it. When you come across an assignment that you are not sure of, just reach for help and your request will always be answered, for you are the Truth of I Am."

"I understand, Teacher. Supporting each soul on its road to individual life satisfaction and completion will aid not only that human, but the entire matrix of the universe because the foundations of the matrix of the universe lie in each individual soul performing its chosen path of primary importance and in developing recognition and support in children's purposes.

"In order to not only aid in universal advancements at rates far greater than has ever been experienced before, but also to help remove the blanket of gloom that seems to keep many humans entrapped and unfulfilled, we attempt to help souls retain knowledge of what they entered their human lives to accomplish. To support universal advancement, we also attempt to help humans to understand the vitally important role that recognizing and supporting other humans' individual purposes plays, no matter how foreign the other roles may seem or how differently other humans speak or act or think from their own line of reasoning."

"Yes, Beautiful Soul, you are wise with this lesson as well. Though this information has been taught to you before, the importance needs repeating for complete absorption. Supporting, following, and promoting individuals on their purpose path and with their truths of being would propel not just the human realm forward, but the universe and beyond, thrusting advancements forward at rates not yet calculable.

"The last of the three-part lesson I will teach you is an important component in the All of the Now. This teaching reveals the third reason that humans do not reach out to us and seek higher consciousness. Many humans spend much of their effort concentrating on one small thing in relationship to life and eternity, clinging to it, holding it in fear of losing it while the massive abundance in all that is and will be is within their reach. In this way they make choices that will affect not only them but all that is within the life experience at hand. Obsessed with the small item they hold so securely in their grasp, they become fixated on it, despondent, and blinded. When they move back from the item they were so afraid of losing, they will then be able to see clearly the item they clung to with such vigor. In the muted reality of focusing on the small instead of the large, they will see it for the value of what it really is compared to what is at stake. Another aspect of the lesson is for every action, there is a reaction. When humans are blinded by the glow of something, whether that be money, advancement, or notoriety, they become mesmerized, worshipping the item as though it were God. They are not open to seeing all the ramifications of their limited vision and actions and are not open to receiving the plethora that is. These humans keep their minds clouded with thoughts of lack, instead of abundance, creating in some cases, wrongs against other humans in an effort to hold closely that which they are obsessed with. They do not realize for the most part that their actions are creating irrevocable harm and that the item they deem more worthy than others can easily be lost, hence losing not only their self-appointed mission of importance but also harming all around them in doing so.

"On another spectrum of this scale are those humans who gather and collect and feel an innate need to hold closely to them as many material items as they can, choosing to focus their attention on filling their lives with substances that satisfy the image of success and happiness. Inside these humans still yearn for a sense of contentment and gratification. Not understanding why they continue to feel lonely and unfulfilled, they gather more material objects and experience the instant, yet temporary, high that those articles create. This is a vicious circle that keeps these humans dazed in a cloud of disconnect from their truths. It keeps them from realizing the missing components of happiness that they are seeking can be found permanently within, not without. There is a difference between gluttony and abundance; when one focuses on abundance, he allows the numbers to fall off. When one focuses on one's truths and purposes for a lifetime, the beauty of true inner joy and peace is experienced.

"Just as with all lessons, life is a balance of all that creates the harmony needed to move forward without the disruptions created by being out of balance. We in the Angelic and Master Realms are determined to spread a dusting of enlightenment on the human realm that will show them the results of false worship and limited thinking. We are allowing them to see all the results of one activity and in doing so, we will enable them to consciously make decisions that will create a positive vibration, instead of a negative vibration."

"There is much that we need to do in the human realm to ensure humans' consciousness assimilates this new earth energy. Where, or rather how, do we help with these lessons, Teacher?"

"We start at the beginning, just as with everything, Beautiful Soul, at the beginning, with each Golden Soul that is welcomed into the human realm. Via messages that are integrated into the humans' daily life, we also aid parents, families, and associates with the vitally important message of allowing individual character to shine brightly. When you help one human understand this, truth rings clearly within him or her and that person will spread the information; and then those who receive it will also spread the information and so forth. It will take all of us with all our reaches to saturate earth's consciousness with the importance of this behavior."

"Beautiful Soul, come with me now. We have a new assignment. This one will not require us to travel to the human realm for administration. This is an assignment that we conduct remotely from here in the Angelic realm. We are going to communicate remotely with an Earth Angel. We will send a message to an Earth Angel's subconscious that he will be called on and have an opportunity to provide assistance."

"Teacher, how do we send a remote communication to the human realm, to an Earth Angel?"

"I will teach you a new skill on this assignment. Sometimes we must help humans to be more aware of their surroundings and to help them feel the needs of other humans. You are about to observe this assignment from the viewpoint of the humans' experience.

"This is a lesson that you have been taught, Beautiful Soul. I will remind you again of this lesson, because it is an important lesson that warrants repeating so that you may fully embrace its meaning and therefore the multitude of uses.

Have Faith.
Think it, Feel it, Sense it
and
It Is."

"Yes, Teacher, I do recall this lesson. I am sorry to make you repeat it. In thinking a thought and then taking action on the thought it will be. We will send a thought to the Earth Angel; the Earth Angel will feel it and then have a sense of what he needs to do and then it will be. Is that correct, Teacher?"

"Yes, Beautiful Soul, that is correct. I will now send a transmission via thought to the Earth Angel that will be involved with our assignment. You will feel this process and sense the diffusion, in doing so you will be able to conduct this type of communication yourself when an assignment calls for it."

"Teacher, how does an Earth Angel know that it has received information from us?"

"That is a good question, Beautiful Soul. The transmission will be received by Earth Angels differently depending on the degree of higher consciousness they have opened themselves up to. Some will receive the message as though they have had an idea of their own, as though they themselves thought of doing a particular act. Earth Angels that have higher conscious thinking will understand that they have been sent a message from Divine and that they are to act on it. We have spoken before of the varying level of consciousness in the human realm. The way the transmission will be received by an Earth Angel is something we are not certain of; we focus on the receipt of communication and that it is acted upon."

Their[5] eyes burned as the sweat rolled down their foreheads and into their eyes. None of them was excited about the move back; they had loved the climate, friends, and lifestyle of their last home. Their new location held a lot of the unknown, except for the weather, which was known to be exceptionally wet. Sometimes life's plans are driven by another set of hands and the best thing to do is be the humble passenger. Thus was their case. They were humbly receiving whatever direction was now given them.

Packing for the move had not been an easy assignment either. As is typical, things that one does not like or does not want to do can easily be put off until absolutely necessary. As a result, boxes were still being packed, shelves cleared, and furniture wrapped when the trucks arrived. The help of friends made the arduous task of loading a bit easier with. Even though, it was still exhausting: lifting, walking up and back down the ramp an uncountable number of times. The two large moving trucks were finally packed to the brim, and they waved good bye to all they loved and motored up the road to what was to be.

Over a thousand miles later, the weary threesome- mom, dad and daughter- pulled the trucks

[5] Cross refer to real-life Angel story 5.

onto the road in front of their new home. With proficient, but tentative maneuvering, the first truck was backed up the steep driveway that lead to the house they would now call home. Traversing the entrance to the home with its perpendicular razorblade stairs leading to the front door was as arduous as getting into the driveway. They would have to unload and carry the contents of each of the two large moving trucks through the rain and up the stairway, a grueling task for professional movers, let alone a mom, dad, and young daughter. Their legs began to feel like rubber as they walked up and down the ramp, up and down the long set of stairs. After they emptied the first truck, the family breathed a silent thank you to God for giving them the strength their weary bodies needed.

The second copiously packed truck was skillfully backed into place and its back door rolled open. Behind the door was another daunting load of boxes and furniture. They all inhaled deeply at the sight. The rain continued to pelt their faces as they painstakingly lifted each piece of furniture and each box down out of the truck, then carried it up the steep split staircase to the house. By this time, wetness had penetrated every layer of clothing; but knowing darkness was drawing near and not wanting to attempt manipulating the truck ramp and stairs in the dark, they pushed forward. Finding fortitude in places they didn't know existed, they muscled each article up and into the house, leaving one piece for last. At the very back of the truck was the double-door, stainless-steel refrigerator. Thankful it was their last piece, yet unsure whether they had the strength to move another item, they robotically progressed, strapping the heavy appliance to the small dolly. They wiggled the toes of their numb feet to help the circulation before beginning the last trek. Down the ramp the heavy refrigerator rolled, bouncing as it hit the gravel driveway. With full might they pushed the wheels of the hand-truck to the stairs. The wheels did not roll; they simply rammed forward creating a clear track where they had been, propelled by the sheer force applied behind the hand truck. Once to the stairs, the exhausted crew could see that the hand cart would not work. They would have to carry the refrigerator up the stairs. Their bodies were nearly trembling from the taxing exertion they had already undergone. Their muscles were still sore from loading all the items into the truck. Now they were being pummeled again, but this time neither the elements nor the architecture was cooperating. A step at a time, they lifted with all their might, wincing with pain. They made it to the turn in the stairs; and, with a thud, the last exertion jammed the refrigerator between the railing of the bottom and top set of stairs. They pushed and pulled, but the appliance did not even wiggle. They knew that to continue up any further they would have to lift it up to completely clear the railing. She could hear her husband ahead of her, hidden by the refrigerator, directing them to count to three and on three they would lift.

The thought of having to hoist the refrigerator anymore, let alone the height required to clear the railings, was overwhelming and brought tears to the woman's eyes. She quietly placed her head against the refrigerator calling for help. Calling on the one thing that she knew would Grace strength to the weak, she prayed. She heard her husband begin the countdown as she completed her prayer. Tightening her muscles in readiness for the last number called, she was prepared to lift with the fury of someone with a fresh breath of resilience. She kept her eyes closed thinking it would help. Just as her husband began to say three, a voice entered their space. It was a male voice. The woman opened her eyes, and next to her stood a man. He smiled at her.

"I have been watching you unload; can't believe you three were able to do so much. That's a lot of stuff you have here. Looks like you could use some help with this refrigerator. Do you mind if I help you with it? The woman nearly cried again, this time for joy in answer to her prayer. The man was strong and lifted the appliance with ease out of its position and up the remainder of the stairs to their new home.

You never know when you will be touched by the help of an Angel, but you do know that when you ask for help, you will receive it in some form.

"Do you see, Beautiful Soul, what was accomplished here?"

"Yes, Teacher, I do. You were able to help this family with strength beyond their own knowledge or imaginings and, when they thought they had no more to give, you showed them that help is just a prayer away. You helped the Earth Angel, the man, to see that he would be a better human by giving of himself to help this family. You helped this man perform an Earth Angel role. You showed each of them to humbly receive and appreciate all the good that life has to offer in every experience, in every moment. You taught them that when they are steered in the direction of their truths and purpose path for their lives, then they will have aid when they need it."

"Yes, Beautiful Soul, that is all correct. Humans being aware and helping other humans spreads a positive vibration in the human realm. The more positive vibrations that are spread, the less room there will be for negative vibrations. It is our job to help humans feel good about helping one another and to be Earth Angels to one another. This gives them a sense of accomplishment and love for their own actions. When they feel this, they will want to serve more. When they help someone with this positive love vibration, that person will in turn, help someone else and will continue passing this torch of *the helping light of love*. In this assignment we see the human who helped the family feel very good about his actions. He is glowing with goodness now, and that goodness will be felt by those he interacts with. In turn, the family knows the strength of prayer and of humbly receiving the help sent in response to that prayer. They will spread that energy with all they meet. We are here to aid in lessons of the great Love of Divine. In every assignment we are given, we will share this important message in different ways, but at the heart it will always be the same message, the message of Love.

"Now, Beautiful Soul, watch another Earth Angel literally step forward with light when responding to a Divine nudge.

The[6] night air chilled their sunburned skin, but it was better to take care of this now than to do it during the precise daylight hours that could be spent having fun. After a little negotiating, they determined who got to stay behind at the campsite and who had to take the boat across the lake to fetch more gas. One of the choices was an easy one because it was Matt's boat and truck. He would drive the boat, park it on the other side of the lake, drive to the neighboring town to fill up the gas cans, drive back to the boat, and motor across the lake to camp. The big debate was who got to stay at camp and who had to ride with Matt and sit in the boat to guard it while Matt drove to town. The short straw went to Roger. Gary and Sam were awarded camp position with the only task of lighting a sizeable campfire- a fire substantial enough that Matt and Roger would be able to easily find their way back to camp in the dark. Gary and Sam were excited with the opportunity to fuel the fire, as well as themselves, while Roger trotted after Matt.

As the boat raced across the water headed toward the dock, the sprays of water added to the chill on their skin, but neither made a visible reaction. Matt made good time driving to town and filling up the cans. He

[6] Cross refer to real-life Angel story 6.

decided to pick up some other provisions as well, those deemed necessary to ensure a fun conclusion to their already successful trip. Roger had brought along some "liquid company" to help hasten time while waiting. That simple addition aided his participation greatly. Sure enough, as Matt pulled back into the boat ramp parking lot, there sat Roger bobbing back and forth in the boat, this time with an even bigger grin than the one he was wearing when Matt left. The gas and provisions were loaded into the boat and the engine was set full blast ahead.

By this time the temperature change had created a low-lying fog across the top of the water making visibility near impossible. The fog actually acted like a mirror when the running lights bounced against it. Matt opted to turn off the lights to improve the visibility, knowing that all he and Roger had to look for was the huge roaring fire that Gary and Sam were tending for them. The moon was just a sliver in the sky and did not penetrate the low fog to help illuminate the lake and banks as it had some times. Still Matt and Roger kept the motor revved and shot onward watching for the fire.

Off to the side they saw a small light, not nearly the size of the campfire they were expecting. Not knowing if they were back yet or not, Matt turned off the engine. The light they saw was actually a lantern being waved back and forth on the bank. "Stop, do not go further! You are out of lake!" a voice bellowed through the fog. Matt turned on the running lights. Just yards ahead of the boat were huge stumps jetting out of the shallow water. Sure enough, they were out of lake. Somehow they had motored past their campsite. They turned around and saw a small-sized fire sparking on the bank. They slowly moved toward the fire. Sure enough it was Gary and Sam. What looked like a large enough fire to them did not appear that big through the fog that encased the lake. Matt and Roger docked the boat and explained to their friends the nearly disastrous event that was prevented by the neighboring camp.

"Beautiful Soul, come with me now. I need to teach you a tool of enlightenment and complete connectivity for a human. We use these tools when the human is ready to approach a new level of insight and to prepare them for their Earth Angel role. You can move on your own now through the veils to the human realm, you no longer need to shift within my field."

"As you wish, Teacher, I will trace your moves." She felt the tingling sensation around her. She sensed her teacher preparing for the energy shift also. She sensed her teacher's progression of interchange from the Angelic realm to the human realm and She mirrored the passage. Though the movement between realms is nearly instantaneous, there is a second or two of intuitive recollection, beginning with a sense of completeness and one with all, through a sense of void, to a sense of singleness, almost loneliness- the last being the feeling in the earth realm. Humans often feel alone, even though they are together. All souls come from the place of unity with and of the universe and from pure acceptance of all that is. This wisdom is in the nucleus of all souls; and though hidden from conscious observation while in the human realm, its loss is unwittingly mourned while in the human realm.

Familiar[7] with this unmistakable sense, She knew they had arrived at their assignment. They were again in a home, a room of the home, a bedroom. Their Angel proficiencies avail them the capability of identifying all human conditions, circumstances, and surroundings. In a breath they are able to feel, smell, see, and hear everything involved in the moment. These abilities assisted in immediate recognition of this assignment as well.

---

[7] Cross refer to real-life Angel story 7.

The thin slice of moon dimly lit the sky and surroundings, creating shadowy illusions of figures everywhere. They were not distracted. There was just one being of energy in the room that required their assistance. There was a woman lying face down on the bed. There was much movement around the woman, but her human vessel was not moving. The movement was coming from images floating above the woman's body. The images of activity were similar to sparks not igniting, to strands of wires stretching up searching for connection but flaying around with no success. As they watched, the activity for connectivity increased.

"Do you understand what is happening here, Beautiful Soul?"

"Teacher, I do not know what is happening. It is as though the woman is reaching for something, attempting to get something, attempting to go somewhere; but her desire and ability are not linking. It is as if her thoughts or sub-conscious is attempting to network with things out of her reach. What does this mean, Teacher?"

"You are correct, Beautiful Soul; her being is leading her on a path to bond with more than is currently part of her realized knowingness. This woman will need help to make the bridge and bond this time. Until this human knows the feeling of binding with information to help her elevate her levels of higher consciousness, we will assist her. All humans have the ability to connect to the truths of the universe. The missions that the soul chose to work on in its current human life determine the information that is available for them to tap into. Since many humans keep this sacred information hidden in places that they cannot readily see or easily remember, they initially require aid to open the doors of this innate knowledge. You see how her subconscious is taking her on a journey? Transporting her on a path? Do you see as she moves along that there is a yearning for more information. . .the cables extending from her, moving around her in search of something, in search of more, in search of enlightenment? Do you see how the cables are sparking to make light, attracting light, bringing to them more light to help the human raise her own light and thus enlightenment? This human knows instinctively what to do, to search for the information; she just does not remember the feeling of connection to Divine knowledge and to the opening of her hidden truths. We are here to help her remember that feeling, that sense of connection. Once a human is able to remember this sense, he or she will never forget it and will welcome every opportunity given to reach for more knowledge and a heightened sense of self truths and higher cognizance, of elevated mindfulness."

"Why do the humans hide away their own truths and ability for furthered advancement if they themselves chose the information to be intertwined throughout their being? It does not make sense that they would hide this raised consciousness from themselves. Why does this happen, Teacher?"

"You are correct, Beautiful Soul, it does not make sense that anything would hide from itself something that would make it better, conceal things that would project it forward to the destination it wants for itself, its chosen and hand-picked purposes and truths. The human realm has the most difficulty with this. Unfortunately, the human realm, for all the brilliance and beauty that it possesses, resonates with some lower energies that keep it distracted from the actualities of greatness. I am not saying that all humans keep themselves distracted from their own truths, but many do. There are reasons that the humans do this; it is not all intentional neglect of Divine promise. They feel disconnected and then feel as though they need to protect themselves, forgetting that there is no greater protection than shining the light of the Divinely blessed truths they brought to their lives. That is part of our mission: to help humans see the beauty that they are and not close that beauty off from being visible to others. On each of them we are to shine the light so brightly that they can no longer hide behind shadows of what cannot be, but instead must move out and soak in the Divine light of all that is. We bring illuminating light that chases away the darkness of lower and negative energies of resistance and complacencies. You see, Beautiful Soul, energies like doubt, fear, lack of self-worth, ignorance of who they truly are, lack of recognition, lack of acceptance, judgment, and sadness seem to run rampant and multiply quickly in the human realm. Humans become familiar with these energies that seem to have created an invisible cloak that has slowly covered them, and they can no longer see anything but the darkness the cloak creates. Too tired to fight against the heaviness, humans resign themselves to what has happened and learn to live in the darkness. Many humans forget that they have the right to live in the warm light of Divine acceptance and unlimited forward progression. Some humans remember. Just as this human we are here to help now remembers. She is searching for the memories of her Divinely blessed greatness. She is searching for her Truth of Being. She is continuously sending out the waves to search for connection but has forgotten the last step: how to connect to Divine knowledge and thus enlightenment. We need to help her remember this last step. We need to fill her with the truth of herself, so she will never forget and so she will be washed with the light of her own brilliant purpose and truths."

They watched the woman search for answers both mentally and physically. Her subconscious mind continued shooting up the cords searching for connectivity. Her physical body rested as its actions continued via thought forms floating above her. She moved in ways that her thoughts recognized as searching. They could see the images the woman was seeing. They could see the physical search mediums the woman was familiar with utilizing in her awake state. First the woman used an automobile as though she were driving to locate something; however realizing the automobile was not efficient alone, she added another search device she was familiar with, a computer exploration device that many humans use in quest of items they seek. They continued to watch as the woman persistently, yet unsuccessfully, maneuvered the representations that she was fixated on, using the images she was familiar with in the physical world, forgetting that searching for aid in the non-physical world required a different action. The woman had forgotten this because she was just beginning to awaken the possibilities of connectivity on all levels. Realizing that effective attempts at locating desired information were eluding her, she changed her means of passage. Engaging the automobile in its typical state, she again maneuvered herself, more easily this time, altering her direction. In front of her was an opening, as though she were approaching a tunnel. Inside the tunnel, instead of the archetypal darkness, radiated an illumination so brilliant she squinted. It felt familiar. She attempted to move toward the tunnel of light, negotiating her vehicle, her mind and her body engaged simultaneously and in unison. The distance to her target did not lessen, despite her negotiations. Though the woman could see her desired destination and she could feel herself involved in the piloting, she was making no additional progress.

"Do you know why the woman cannot advance to her desired terminus, Beautiful Soul?"

"It feels as though there is something missing with the woman, Teacher. As though she is working hard to achieve something but does not have the complete ability to do it."

"You are correct, Beautiful Soul. The woman has her mind and her body engaged to orchestrate something; however, she does not have her soul in line with the process. To have the ability to achieve a chosen outcome, everything- mind, body and soul- need to be engaged and in line for the common goal. Do you know how to help her? Do you feel what to do?"

"I believe I do, Teacher. . .I do know how. . .I do know how to wash her with the greatness that she is." At that She moved over the woman and touched the fingers of her right hand to the base of the woman's neck. There was a swirl of energy; brilliantly flashing light sparkled its way into the woman's neck. Then She pulled the woman to her and held her in a vertical position. The woman's crown chakra opened to Divine as She allowed the light to register throughout the woman's being, through every molecule, through every cell. Through mind, body and soul the warming light of pure love washed her, chasing away the darkness that shadowed her own truths, swirling through her like an impenetrable syrup of Divine enrichment. The woman glowed giftedly. When the light was fully accepted

Page 181

by the woman, She slowly rested her back on the bed, laying her down on her stomach again, allowing the woman to integrate all the truths that she had just allowed to awaken within herself. The woman was entranced with the intensity created by this showering of unification, and her body pulsed as the knowledge and communication surged through her and charged her mind, body and soul, melding them together. Gradually the truths were assimilated into her being and she rested quietly, still absorbing, still registering truths, and still radiating from the Divine gift.

"You have done well, Beautiful Soul. This human soul is now registering at a much higher frequency and is now able to call forward the truths of her own being. Look at the peace in which she is resting as her being recognizes the presence of the Divine that she knows but had forgotten. It will take her a while to call it all forward; she had hidden much away, as many in this realm do. The glow inside this human is beautiful and will light the way for many other humans now. That is how we are to help this realm- by opening the humans up to their own Divine light so they can operate at the vibration that they are intended to in this life, allowing them to have their own sight of truths and purpose, allowing them to see themselves for the first time in many years, perhaps the first time since they were born."

"Teacher, how do we know that this human will not forget the lesson that we just bestowed upon her?"

"That is something we do not know. If she falters again, then we will aid her in recognition; and we will continue to do so until she no longer needs intervention. We will all sing praises for humans who work hard to realign themselves with the truths and purposes that they were born with. When we raise consciousness levels, then it affects not just the soul that was ministered to, it inspires all the beings that soul comes into contact with. A wave of knowledge creates a larger wave of knowingness."

Chapter Seven

The Lesson of Realm Contributions

and

Multiple Now's

"Come,[8] Beautiful Soul, we have another

assignment. Remember when I told you there are times that

we receive assignments from the department that monitors human purpose paths and truths? We have just received an assignment from that department. We must act fast, Beautiful Soul. Come to me now and let us shift realms."

As the white sparkling film of mist dissipated, they found themselves inside a home, looking on where a family had gathered around a long table decorated handsomely and covered with mountains of food. The smells were intoxicating.

"I had forgotten this, the breathtaking smells of food, the taste of food, both good and bad." She allowed the smells to fill her.

"Yes, the human realm for all the bad it must endure, has magnificent things that we shall never sample again, a holiday feast being one of them. We are able though to open our senses and call back all the sensations of experiences that we had in the human realm. So, for every assignment and every human life that you lived, you will be able to call upon the senses that were awakened and used."

As they looked on enjoying the family in full merriment and feasting, they could not help but smile. "It is

---

[8] Cross-refer to real-life Angel story 8.

so satisfying to see such happiness and harmony within the human realm. Our wish is that all humans experience such warm, pure love."

"Step by step, Teacher, I guess that is what we do, step by step, sharing the love and light in all ways that we know how."

"That is right, Beautiful Soul. Those are the gifts that we bring to share. It is time for us to step in now, Beautiful Soul. We must help one of these humans." She watched as her teacher moved around the table and gently positioned her finger, almost touching the temple of all but one human seated at the table. With this, the disposition of the conversation changed to one of a more serious nature. All the humans that the teacher had touched united and began questioning the untouched human about his health. Each of the united humans insisted and persisted until the untouched human finally agreed to see a doctor.

She looked at the untouched human and then She felt him. There was a problem with this gentleman. She could feel a problem within him. "He needs to see the doctor immediately, Teacher, I can feel that he does."

"Yes. Beautiful Soul, he does." They continued watching as the families concluded their evening together and dispersed to their own homes to recharge. She and her teacher followed the gentleman to his home and, just before he fell to sleep, the teacher placed her finger on his temple. A purple light flashed when she touched him. The gentleman's body jerked but then fell to sleep. They waited by his bed as he and his wife slept. "Humans need to award their bodies sleep to reclaim their energy. The human body undergoes much and requires adequate sleep to carry on. We will wait with these humans until they have satisfied this obligation."

As the sun rose and filled the sky with colors of red, orange, rose, and yellows, so too did the humans rise. In a scurry to prepare for their day's requirements, they all leapt into their everyday routine, except for the gentleman. After showering and dressing and before leaving for work, he satisfied the promise he had made to his family the night before; he called his doctor and explained to him the symptoms he had been suffering with over the last several weeks.

"Come, Beautiful Soul, we must move locations." With that, they shifted simultaneously into a different location, a doctor's office. She watched the doctor as he shuffled papers on his desk while he carried on a conversation over speaker phone. She watched as Teacher put her finger to, but not touching, the doctor's temple.

His hands stopped rearranging; he altered his full attention to the phone. The doctor looked directly at the phone and continued listening, now more intently, to the gentleman's descriptions. The doctor expressed his strong desire for the gentleman to make an appointment with his office that day. He placed the man on hold to transfer him to the receptionist to make an appointment.

The receptionist answered and unfortunately reported that they had no open appointments that day. She watched as her teacher put her finger to the receptionist's temple but did not touch it. Instantaneously the receptionist stopped and changed her statement, I am sorry, I was mistaken, we do have time this morning, please come right in.

The gentleman called his work and told them that he would be late and then proceeded to his appointment. It took the doctor minutes to pin-point the problem. The gentleman was admitted immediately to the hospital and scheduled for surgery.

"You see, Beautiful Soul, we had to change the direction for this human because the path that he was on was not in alignment with his purpose path and truths."

"Teacher, what were you doing with your finger? With each family member, the doctor, and the receptionist you almost touched their temple, but did not; however you touched the gentleman's temple. When you touched the gentleman, there was a spark of purple light. Why did you touch one and not all?"

"I simply gave a feeling of intensity to the family members when they talked to the gentleman about his health and also interjected to insist that he see the doctor soon. I knew they would talk about his health because he had not been feeling well for some time, but I needed to interject in each of them a very urgent feeling for action so they would passionately speak to him to seek help. With the doctor, and then the receptionist, I simply allowed them to see that they did have room in the morning to see someone who was desperately in need of the doctor's help. I made them feel the magnitude of the situation."

"How about the gentleman before he fell to sleep? What was the purple light?"

"I touched the gentleman with pure love and light and gave him a purple healing flame to keep him safe until he was able to see the doctor the following day. You can do all of these things, Beautiful Soul- healing, providing extended sight and ideas, and much more. Just feel it and it will be. You will be able to practice these tools soon."

"I trust you teacher, but you have shared so much with me today. I will maintain the Faith that I can do all that you teach me and all that is Divinely required in each situation for each assignment."

"That is good. Our work here is done, we may leave now."

"I would like to do one more thing if I may, Teacher."

"Certainly, Beautiful Soul."

This time the teacher followed as She led her into another room of the hospital. In this room they saw a woman on her knees weeping and praying, pleading with God to save her beloved son for the sake of his children, his wife, the family, and for her. If he were to pass, the hole from his loss would be too large to fill, the pain too great. She looked to the heavens and smiled. The room was instantly filled with warmth and Divine love. Keeping her eyes affixed on the heavens, She placed her hand on the woman's left

Page 191

shoulder, allowing the Divine warmth and love to radiate through the woman.

Then a voice came from the Heavens directed to the woman, "He Is Strong." The woman shuddered and began to rise. The voice that answered her prayers left her feeling encouraged and humble. When the woman was completely standing, her head still lifted to Heaven, She took her Angel Wing and waved it through the woman's being, releasing any fears, worries and doubts.

"Now we are done here," She said turning her gaze to her teacher. The teacher glowed from the connection of miracles she had just observed.

"Beautiful Soul, this human will need us again. This will be a double assignment. You will go to her again."

"When, Teacher, and why?"

"Beautiful Soul, you will know when you will feel this human call for assistance again. Just like all whom you help, there may be a time when the human will call again to request aid with something. It is always a pleasure to see and feel and recognize a human whom you have visited before, to be able to assist a human that you are acquainted with and to feel how he or she is able to recognize Angelic intervention quicker than the first time we were called to be of assistance.

We are, however, able to see in the future because it is Now. If you would like to try now, you can see in this woman's future, feel when she will require your Divine love again. Open your senses to know when she will need you."

"Teacher, I do not know this lesson. Seeing forward? Seeing in the future at a time not Now so that I may help someone?"

"Yes, Beautiful Soul, remember the lesson of time? That all time is Now? Past is Now, Future is Now and Present is Now. Put yourself in that knowingness concept. Let that truth flow over you and through you as though warm syrup were running through your being. When you are able to experience all that is at the same time, then you will be able to direct your attention and give help to situations in any Now- past, future or present."

"That is a foreign thought to me, Teacher. To be somewhere other than here at the same time I am here?"

"Yes, Beautiful Soul, to be omnipresent. I want you to feel the multiple Now. You can help this woman at this time and with a future requirement. Release all else and feel this woman's future need."

She[9] followed her teacher's instructions, releasing any questions that had arisen during the introduction of this lesson and allowed herself to open to the idea of being in this woman's multiple reality times- past, present and future- all at once. She felt nothing. She centered herself and gave full intention to the lesson. She gave intention to being at this woman's future assignment. Slowly a vision came to her; then more than a vision, a full sense enveloped her. She was in a room, in the kitchen of this woman's home. The woman stood alone, pouring herself a cup of coffee. The smells of the brewing coffee awakened her senses. The woman was happy and sad at the same time. The day was her celebration of life day. Her day to celebrate coming to the life she was in. A day specially selected by her prior to entering this realm to make a difference and perform her chosen purposes. It is a day every human should celebrate because they have a chance to make significant contributions to the whole of humanity and to the universe. This woman had forgotten this truth, as many do. She was sad and feeling alone. By herself on her day of celebration, she felt a longing for belonging.

---

[9] Cross-refer to real-life Angel story 9.

She could feel the sadness in the woman. She sent a call to the great Knowingness of all that is. She asked that this woman's parents be summoned, so that they could be with her. Within moments, She sensed the two important beings with her and with the woman. She wrapped her wings around the woman and the two important beings merged into the wings, melting, and intertwining themselves. The woman's energy changed. The woman was filled with all Divine light as she was able to feel the presence of her loved ones aided by the Angel. She watched as the woman, still wrapped within her wings, grew cheerful and felt loved,. She watched as the parents glowed with the love they shared with the woman. The room began to illuminate from all the love that was shared within those moments. Slowly the parent beings pulled away, leaving pure essence of constant love with the woman. She pulled her wings away simultaneously. The woman radiated. The woman would never feel complete aloneness again because she had been gifted the awareness of the Divine blessing of eternal love.

"You did well with the assignment of multiple Now's drawn into one. As I taught, this will be a lesson that you will utilize with various assignments. Always remember that there is no time, it is all Now.

"Beautiful Soul, I will present you with another monitoring opportunity. I need you to tune into a scene in the human realm. It is one that we will be monitoring. We will lend our assistance much with this assignment. It is not a one-time assignment like the others have been; this is an assignment that will require our monitoring and help periodically. Each of these humans has a special role in this, and we need to help them stay focused with their truths. Our first assignment will be to help this young woman with strength as she engages in the task of releasing a new Golden Soul into its human life. The entry of the Golden Soul will be difficult on the young woman; we will need to be with her at that time."

"Do we go now, Teacher?"

"No, we will both sense when it is time to join them. Until then I want you to tune in to their energies and know who they are, feel who they are. In doing so you will sense when it is time."

"Who am I to feel? How many are you referring to teacher?"

"Feel, Beautiful Soul; allow your senses to open to the assignment. You will have the answers when you release yourself to all the knowledge that is making itself available to you."

The woman's face was lightly wrinkled, but her smile exposed each line beautifully as she cooed and cawed in glee at the new baby girl lying peacefully in her bassinette. Standing next to her was the baby's momma, glowing with love as new mothers do.

"She is beautiful, what a wonderful addition to our family. You can almost see her heart glowing through her clothes. She is a very special little girl," Janie smiled up at her niece. "Truthfully your delivery had me quite alarmed, though I did not want to react negatively at the time. The baby came so quickly, before anyone was ready really, before your mother could be here with you. The doctor could not believe you were dilated as much as you were when we arrived at the hospital. The bed-rest you had been on generally regulates delivery time, but it did not seem to play a role in your timeline or should I say baby Abigail's timeline. That exquisite little girl was ready to make her presence known and to join her new life," Janie said laughingly, then again became serious, "Your back created such immobility for adjusting the correct posture of the baby. At one point I saw the doctor's face as he looked at the

Page 197

nurse. To tell you the truth I thought there was something seriously wrong; but then, in an instant, things changed; and there was your beautiful baby girl, exposing herself to the world and softly crying. It is the first time I have witnessed such a blessed event. Thank you for allowing me to be there with you. I feel bad my sister was not, but blessed that I was!"

"Thank you, for being here, Auntie. I truly loved having you here by my side; it just seemed to keep me at peace. In fact, through all the scurrying, whispering, and skeptical looks, I was not nervous or afraid; I just had this peace over me like everything was going to be okay, like I was being held. I just do not know how else to put it. It does break my heart that I cannot be with her for a while though. This dang back of mine. Wouldn't you know I am going to need surgery again, now of all times, with a new baby?"

"We are lucky that you were able to deliver without incident, considering how screwed up your spine is. That blessing is what you need to focus on. Remember Abigail will be in good hands with me; you do not need to be concerned about that. Just wrap her with your love and that will last her a lifetime."

"Yes, you are right, Auntie. It is just hard. I want to hold her and kiss her constantly. But you are right; I am so blessed to have a successful delivery and a beautiful daughter."

The two women stood silently smiling at the sleeping baby, transfixed by the miracle before them.

Finally Janie broke the silence, "You know your mother will want to spend time with her too. When did Rachel say she would be here? Between the two of us, thanks to our varied outlooks, Abigail will have a wonderfully broad vision of life. Little Abigail won't know which way is up with all of us giving our input on life." She laughed at the thought.

"I think it is time for us to say a prayer of gratitude for the gift lying here before us, a gift that has been delivered to all of us really." The women bowed their heads as Janie, a minister for many years, lead them in a prayer of gratitude. Just as they finished, the door behind them was flung open and with a crash hit the wall. The two women shifted their gaze to see who had caused such a racket in the room of a sleeping newborn.

"Rachel, shhhh. Abigail is. . ." Before Janie could complete her scolding, the baby entered the conversation with a shrill cry.

The new mother cringed in pain as she bent over to pick her baby up and then cuddled her close to her chest. "It is feeding time anyway, I guess."

"You have been on your feet too long; let me hold her while you climb back in to bed." Janie held the baby as the new mom with the aid of her own newly arrived

mother painstakingly climbed back into the hospital
bed.

"Oh dear, I am sorry you are in such pain,"
Rachel said, kissing her daughter on the forehead.
"What a blessing my granddaughter is healthy and
beautiful. Though I still cannot believe she did not wait
for me to be here before joining this world. Oh what fun
she and I will have! Sis, it is my turn to hold my
granddaughter, you have had enough time with her,"
she trailed off, smiling and gathering the baby from
Janie's arms.

"Actually it is my turn to hold my baby, it is
feeding time."

"Beautiful soul, I knew that you would sense when
this assignment would need us. You did well holding the
mother's head and sharing pure love with her to keep her
calm and in a state of welcoming gratitude. I had to go to the
new Golden Soul and surround her with the same pure love
from Divine and remind her that it was time to join the new
life she had chosen for herself. I removed all fear and stress
that surrounded the Golden Soul, so she would easily free
herself from the developmental environment she grew in.
You see, Golden Souls become accustomed to the warmth

and unconditional love that they are encased in within the human's body. These Golden Souls are seeds of pure Divine love; this is how they grow within the human's system. The transition from that sacred space to an independent existence can be a difficult evolution. We attempt to always have a Transitional Angel at this juncture to help the new Golden Souls with entry into their human lives, reminding them that their path is one that they chose and that now they are released to begin the journey."

"It is a magnificent assignment to witness such a miracle, Teacher, a seed of Divine light manifesting into a soul in small human form. Thank you for this lesson. I am humbled by witnessing this and by the Heavenly vision our Creator has. Orchestrating hallowed flows of energy throughout the universe, each intertwining with the others to create the picture of each participant's reality is an amazingly complex vision. Realizing now the small field of connectivity between all, I understand the importance of creating triggers to remind every realm of its significant participation in the greater good by helping humans shine their naturally brilliant love light onto others and onto all that is and will be."

"You are very wise, Beautiful Soul. What you say is true; we are honored to be part of the Godly plan. This assignment is not over for us; rather, as I mentioned before, it has just begun. This new Golden Soul will require our participation in her life many times.[10] We will also be called on to remind those around her of their purposes and truths, so that each will remember the importance of spreading their wings to truly shine and allow the new Golden Soul to do the same."

"Teacher, there was mention of different realms in a past lesson: Earth, Nature, Aquatic, and Fairies realms. I feel that I know these realms, but I do not. What are these realms? How do we provide assistance? How do they reciprocate?"

"Beautiful Light, you have learned many lessons of how we gift the human realm. We also provide assistance in different realms—the Earth realm, the Aquatic realm, the Nature realm, even the Fairies realm, those that you ask of, to name a few. I will supply you a brief explanation of these realms. Your assignments will provide more lessons with

---

[10] Cross refer to real-life Angel story 10.

their involvement. Each of these realms grants assistance to all other realms, just as we do. They are part of the entwined mesh of the Divine cosmic plan of multi- alliance dependency and support.

"Pay attention to messages that you receive from these different sources. Cooperation to a common goal is performed much more expeditiously when there is knowingness for such. Every realm has a feature or features that are of particular importance to others.

"The Earth Realm gives the human realm unwavering support and balance. It also provides needed balance to space. The Earth realm contains inanimate objects such as the earth's mountains and rocks, dirt, sand, and comparable elements. These items are living items and part of the Oneness of all that is, but they are not animate as other realms are, so many times they are not recognized for the importance that they contribute. Without the stability, venting, polishing, and pliable base they provide, other realms would not exist.

"The Nature realm is greatly dependent on the earth realm for protection, growth, and nourishment. The Nature realm contains animate objects such as animals, birds, insects, reptiles, and vegetation, to identify a few. It is a very large diverse realm dependent upon itself and the multiplicity of others. Many of the messengers we send to humans are from this realm. We will send a bird or an animal to be seen by a human who does not yet have the sight to see all the other channels of communication they have available to them. We send messages of love, beauty, support, and humor through these messengers as well as through the Aquatic realm. Ascended relatives of humans also send messages via the Nature and Aquatic realms. Many humans see the messenger and feel the message being sent to them from a departed love one, but then discount the event because the human mind is not elevated enough to realize these truths. They approach events that are not easily explainable with the limited logic that they utilize. Though this is changing as a result of the new wave of higher consciousness, it may take some time for all humans to trust in their feelings of things and not over think and discount the very thing that could help them and bring them joy.

"The Aquatic realm contains all water entities. It too is a large, diverse realm containing vertebrate, mammals, plankton, mermaids and mermen, and vegetation. As with all realms, so you are learning, the Aquatic realm is also dependent on other realms for existence. Many times a courier from this realm will deliver communications of love, support and humor. The dolphins are the quintessential example of the realm spreading joy and happiness. Members of this realm exercise high levels of communications that can be interpreted by humans with higher consciousness levels.

"The Fairies realm is the most fanciful of the realms and of the four you are studying in this lesson, it operates at the highest frequency and, therefore, is not as easily visible as the others. This is an active realm with many varied affiliates though named for just one. The realm of Elementals contains Fairies, Gnomes, Elves, Brownies, Leprechauns, Sprints, Devas, and Pixies among others. Inhabitants of this realm can shape shift, if they so desire, to be visible to lower frequency realms, such as the human realm. As an example, a fairy can become a dragonfly to allow transference of messages through subconscious channels to lower-frequency recipients.

"A very important thing for all souls to know and remember is to honor everything. Just as a soul elected to enter the human realm to perform assignments that are based on human contributions, so do other souls enter other realms based on the greatness of All that Is. A soul may enter as a human's pet dog or pet cat, their purpose being to heal and bring humor, companionship, and more. These souls that have chosen to enter in anything that supports the drive to Divine greatness must be monitored. I have observed some human's treat their pets from the Nature realm with disregard, unloving, not realizing that the pet is a soul that could very well have been an Angel in a past life. These souls have chosen a life of service at great sacrifice, not knowing what their life encounters will be. Honor everything, for everything is of value and part of Divine.

"Another important thing to remember with all realms, Beautiful Light, is that cooperation and the vision of Oneness is vital to existence, advancement and solidarity. You will know when the realms are to enter an assignment for assistance. You will appreciate what each realm contributes at different intervals. Each is as important as the other because they are all part of the Oneness. Does this information register within your being, Beautiful Light?"

"Yes, Teacher. This is a vast subject. We have many teams of realms, all operating with the same directive."

"That is correct, Beautiful Light. There is support for everyone and everything always."

Chapter Eight

The Lesson of Healings, Oneness, and Tones

"I will teach you of our Angelic realm's healing abilities now. There is a division that works specifically with human realm healings. They are known quite simply as, the Healing Angels. Their purpose is to receive the assignments that require our realms intervention when it pertains to the human vessel healing. You see, sometimes humans allow too much darkness to grow within them and this darkness festers and boils and becomes solid masses of infection. Much too often, this darkness begins with negative emotions that are held onto, instead of released. Many humans brew the negative and lower energies within them, allowing their brewing to boil, spilling out on to themselves and others. Instead of learning the valuable lessons from each encounter and then discarding the negative portion, they hold on to the negative emotions and discard the lesson or dismiss the lesson as irrelevant."

"Beautiful Soul, we have been given another assignment. Join me now; travel with me, but independently. Feel the assignment and where we are to go."

She opened herself to receive the assignment. She felt and She knew. She traveled parallel to her teacher's energy as they shifted realms to their destination.

"Do you know what we are to do here, Beautiful Soul? Do you know what your role is here?"

"Yes, Teacher. I see the woman.[11] I feel that it is not this woman's time yet, though she has a heaviness within her that is burdening her and distracting her from her truths and visions. I see the cause of her pain and how that anguish has

---

[11] Cross refer to real-life Angel story 11.

been allowed to grow within her, to take her over. I see how she is carrying the grief of someone else as though it were hers, letting that sorrow blind and drown her in the darkness. I see how she feels the torment of emotions that are misguided and untrue. She is allowing the actions of others to weigh upon her as though they were her actions, her meaning for life. We need to help this woman realize that it is not her job to carry the consequences of other human's decisions, whether right or wrong. It is only her job to be true to the purposes and truths that are part of her life's journey. We need to help this woman realize that she need only learn from the lessons given to her and not wear the negative emotions like a shroud that stifles the light. This woman feels as though she has been wounded by another human, betrayed, abandoned, and cut to the core. She has allowed those emotions to multiply within her, causing her grave harm. We need to help this woman realize that all humans are responsible for their own actions; and, therefore, her only job is to live the life of her own choices.

"The consequences of an action is a lesson that should be applied to the next step of existence, rather than allowing it to wipe out existence. We need this woman to know that every human soul chooses its own path in each

Page 211

lifetime, each path having a multitude of experiences to learn from and each path moving the soul further on its own independent journey. Though human paths intersect and humans should learn from each other and from their touches on other humans' lives, it is not their job to live life for another, to carry the burdens of life experiences needed by another. We need this woman to remember these truths, so that she can share them with others, so that she can remove the negative bindings that are drowning her, and so that she can shine her light brightly on all she comes in contact with. By her example and teaching, she can help other humans realize the value of lessons; the value of respecting individual lessons and decisions, not living them for another but staying true to the path of self; and the importance of releasing the negative emotions in lessons and holding onto the lesson itself as a gift for advancement."

"You are correct in your assessment. This woman has an important role in this life. It is hers to teach others the truths of independent paths in the convergence of multiple paths. She is to teach others to be true to self and to allow others to learn the needed lessons that they are here to learn without interception, to not carry the burdens for others but to release the negative aspect and highlight the benefits for herself and for others.

Humans, who wallow in the negative emotions of yesterday; holding on to resentment, anger, disappointment, betrayal, sadness, and the like, are not performing at their Divine level for existence. They are not applying themselves to the purpose and truths of being they were born to follow in their lives. They have allowed themselves to become obsessed with wrongs, to be blinded by perceived offenses instead of radiating at a frequency of Divine pure love. We will help cleanse this woman of the darkness that is growing in her, so that she can clearly see Heaven's love. So that she will be witness to Angelic presence and the power of prayer. In turn, she will share this knowledge with others."

"And, Now, Beautiful Light, come with me. We must awaken the senses of an Earth Angel and fill him with directives to accomplish in the assignment we were just given."

"Teacher, I am confused with what it is you say we need to do. Are you saying that we will be working concurrently with an Earth Angel on our assignment?"

"Yes, Beautiful Light, that is what I am instructing you. We will request the assistance of an Earth Angel and present the information to the Earth Angel for his participating role."

"How Teacher, how are we to present an Earth Angel with their agenda of involvement?"

"Patience, Beautiful Light, all information comes in the time it is to come. Pushing and rushing does not change the timeline in which a lesson is to be learned. Those actions simply take up space until the lesson appears to you at the time that was predestined. Do you understand this?"

"Yes, Teacher, I do and I apologize for my insistent behavior. It seems I have many questions, all of which I understand now will be answered in the time that they are to be answered, according to matrix of the experience."

"That is correct with every situation Beautiful Light. With our current assignment, we will support an Earth Angel with behavior that is not generally recognized as Angelic. To accomplish the greatest good, there are times that assertive behavior and unattractive characteristics must present themselves. Such is the case with the assignment for this Earth Angel. Come with me Now."

The swirling of energy enveloped them both and almost instantaneously they were placed in the human realm. Before them lay a man sleeping; next to him was a woman, also recharging her human vessel. The sounds coming from the man caused their feathers to shiver as he exhaled with voluminous roars and growls. She watched as her Teacher moved to the side of the man and placed her finger on his temple. She saw as a bolt of light jetted from her Teacher's finger into the man's head, almost sparking. The man jumped with the action, coughing and gasping, but then relaxed back to the exaggerated breathing he had been demonstrating when they arrived. "We are done here, Beautiful Light. I have given this man the information that he needs to perform this assignment with the attitude and mannerisms that are required. We will monitor this assignment to assure that it is executed correctly. If it is not, then we will visit this loud man again."

Doris[12] pulled the covers tightly around her in an effort to warm herself from the chill that penetrated her very core. She glanced at the clock that sat on the

---

[12] Cross refer to real-life Angel story 12.

nightstand next to her bed, 5:30 a.m. The thought of
getting out of bed, dressing and going to work was
inconceivable, but she simply could not miss another
day. Her boss had made it clear by his tone yesterday
that he was not pleased with her absences. She slowly
worked her way out of the warm covers and slid her
legs to the side of the bed, her feet resting on the floor.
Sluggishly she raised herself to a standing position and
her knees began to buckle. She sat back down. Looking
at the clock again, it was now 5:45. She needed to take a
shower before going to work since she had spent the last
four days in bed without one. Again she attempted to
stand, forcing her legs to be strong and support her
weight; they did, though still shaky. Her breaths were
short and laborious. She felt weak and as though she
could not breathe deeply. She took a step forward and
then another and another until she could rest herself
against the doorjamb leading to the bathroom. By this
time she was breathing exhaustedly, working hard to fill
her lungs with enough air. Her head began to feel light;
she could feel her body swirling. She held on tightly to
the doorjamb until she felt steady enough to move.
Several minutes later, Doris resigned herself to the fact
that she could not make it to the shower, let alone work.
She turned and painstakingly worked her way back to
bed, lowering herself into the warm covers and
wrapping herself up tightly again. Her body trembled.

Page 216

Knowing that her boss would not be in for another hour she allowed herself to drift back to sleep, every breath becoming more peaceful.

She woke with a start, as though someone had shaken her bed. She was immediately aware that she needed to call her boss and let him know that she could not make it in. Five after seven, she was five minutes late. She dialed the number; it rang several times before a deep manic voice answered the phone. Attempting to gather a deep breath and forcing the air into her lungs, she asked to speak with her boss. Minutes later her boss picked up the line and spoke in a hurried, gruff tone. "Yes?"

"Mr. Huff, this is Doris Meyer, I will not be able to come in to work today, I am still ill."

"Ms. Meyer, are you aware how many days you have missed this month?"

"Yes, sir, I am; and I am sorry. I just cannot seem to get out of bed. I am feeling quite poorly, sir."

"Well, then Ms. Meyer, I must insist that upon your return to work, you bring with you a note from your doctor explaining your illness and as a result your inability to come to work," Mr. Huff demanded in an even gruffer tone.

"Yes, sir, I will." Doris hung up the phone breathing heavily again, annoyed that her boss had demanded she visit the doctor before her return to

Page 217

work, annoyed that she was sick in the first place, annoyed that she could barely breathe in deeply enough to fill her lungs. She laid her head back down and gathered the covers up tightly again. In a matter of minutes she was fast asleep and did not wake until 4:45 in the afternoon. The first thoughts on her mind were of the conversation she had with her boss. What an imposing figure, she thought, but like it or not she was going to have to visit her doctor and get a note. Realizing that the doctor's office would close soon, she dialed the office and made an appointment for the following morning at 10:00. Her next call was to her daughter, Judy, to secure a ride, knowing that if tomorrow morning were anything like today, she would be unable to drive herself. After making the necessary arrangements, she drifted back to sleep.

The phone rang shrilly in her ear. Not recognizing the sound at first, she groggily uncovered her head. By the third ring she remembered where she was and answered the phone. It was her daughter. "Mom, where are you? Are you ready? I am here to take you to your appointment."

"Oh my, I am not ready. . .I am still in bed. Use your key and come in. I still have to take a shower."

"Mom, you don't have time; we will be late." By this time, Judy had hung up, unlocked the door, and begun walking and hollering down the hall in the direction of her mom's room. She opened the door to see her mother feebly attempting to stand.

"Mom, what is it? Why didn't you tell me you were so sick? There is no way you can get in the shower. Let me just help you clean up a bit and then we will go." Doris had told Judy about the conversation with her boss the day before, and at the time Judy had been quite irritated with his request. Now seeing the condition of her mother, she thought that perhaps it was not a bad idea at all to have her mother checked by the doctor. Judy helped her mother clean up and dress and then helped her to the car. As they exited the car at the doctor's office and walked in, her mother, through her actions—straightening her posture and walking with deliberate intention— forced strength from a hidden place that Judy had no idea her mother had. Making the pleasantries with the doctor, Doris spoke as though she had been just slightly discomforted by her illness and repeated a couple times that if it had not been for the unfair demands of her boss, there really would be no need for her to have had the appointment.

As the doctor checked her vitals and listened to her lungs, his facial expression changed. His brow furrowed as he moved the stethoscope back and forth from Doris' chest to her back. "I am going to order an x-ray of your lungs, just to make sure we are not missing anything."

"Is there something wrong doctor?" questioned Judy.

"Just want to check on something," he answered, leaving the room.

As soon as the door closed, Doris' posture wilted and she began to breathe shallowly again. "This is silly; I just need some rest."

"Well, Mom, it is good to have the doctor check everything. He has to, you know, if he is going to write you a note for your work," Judy responded with concern encircling her reply.

The door opened to the room and in came a nurse and a wheelchair. "Let's get you down to x-ray, shall we, Hon?" chirped the lively nurse whose hair was the color of mustard.

An hour later, Doris and Judy were back in the patient room waiting for the doctor's report. "This is taking forever," puffed Doris. "A reason right here why I do not like coming to the doctor's office; they make you wait and wait while they help fifteen patients at the same time." Doris abruptly stopped her complaining as the door opened. It was the doctor, followed by a different nurse.

"Mrs. Meyer, the doctor led in a tone more tentative than before, "we have found something in the x-ray." I will need to do further tests, but it appears there may be a condition with your lungs."

All are One and One is All

"Your lesson in this Now is one that you have felt a touch of while studying here, but it is much more valuable and comprehensive than what you have discovered thus far. This lesson, with its straightforward message, we would think to be received and integrated just as easily as others, but it does have a hidden concept challenge for some that spurs a competitive charge of self-dominance. We are aiding in creating a balanced, level, and unthreatening zone for administration, creating a tone that can be understood by all; so that the universal importance of integration will be grasped, appreciated, and interwoven. Do you sense that which I speak of?"

"Teacher, I am sensing this will correlate to the lesson I received when I first woke within this realm of the pure nature and Oneness that I feel from and around everyone. There is a sense of equal, undivided energy and acceptance."

"You have partial sense of this lesson. I will provide you more, so you will contain a wholeness of this intelligence. Just as with the lesson of communication, oneness requires active involvement. The participation needed is one of acceptance that everything and everyone are equal because they are all one thing. Meaning, that all, everywhere, similar and different, are all the same and one.

Everything is One thing.
Everyone is One thing.

"That means that all the realms, no matter how different they appear or feel or operate, are One thing.

"That means that no matter how different the individual things and beings are within each realm, we are all one thing.

"That means that all of us here within this realm are one thing.

You are Me

and

I am You.

"That means all the humans are of us and we are of them. All the realms, whether inanimate or mobile are all of us and we are of them. A rock is of an Angel as a human is of a Master and a butterfly is of a rock and a dolphin is of a planet.

"We are all connected and we are all one thing.

"When the true significance of this truth is communicated and Mastery of this truth is achieved, all will know the importance of their role in the Oneness that is. All will strive to be the best, knowing that they are impacting the balance of what is.

"This actuality will challenge those who allow their egos to govern their thinking in the respect that they believe that they are better than others, better than other humans and better than other realms. The truth of this lesson demonstrates that a speck of dust holds equal value to a human or to a planet because if one were not present the whole would not be complete. Absolute balancing of ego is required when it is known that all are part of One and there is only One.

"Some humans, as you have learned, allow penetration of energies that do not contain properties of composition that are of positive charge. These negatively charged energies create much distraction within and around the vessel they have entered. They will adhere themselves to the human personality creating in some cases, character flaws. Ego is a housing location for negatively charged energies. Ego in itself is not bad because it contributes to the individual sense of worth a human has; however when the ego becomes negatively charged, it expands with the charge and becomes overbearing, placing pressure on things it is in contact with and focusing more attention on the enlarged area and less on others. One can never see clearly when looking through fog.

"When humans do not accept or look for help, then they are letting ego steer them. Therefore, those who struggle with being superior over others or over things have to be aided in the assimilation of the truth of this lesson. That is why we are creating the unchallenging, universally recognized tone for this lesson. The tone will be accepted by the soul because the soul knows Divine and a negatively charged ego will not place the shield of defiance up, which prevents saturation. Administration of the tone is primal; simply thinking creates a tone and so it is. We are sending representatives, as indicated earlier, to areas of need to speak with the Divine souls and allow them to hear the truth of this tone.

"Another element of Oneness and information that is calculated and preserved within the tone is each soul is placed in a vessel of transportation, a physical body in the human realm; and there are requirements for maintenance of this vessel. The unification of the physical vessel, the mind in conjunction to expansion, and their soul in connection to illumination make the whole. Our department must educate the human realm on the importance of *self*-care at the highest of levels because their treatment of self impacts the balance of the realms, the balance of all that is and will be. Since all are one and one is all, the effects of one human's self-care are laminate for another and for the earth and for the waters and for the world and for the universe and for all-encompassing creation. Again, an example of the truth: for every action there is a reaction. When one human does not maintain his or her vessel in highest of regard, whether that be poor diet, abuse of toxic elements, lack of mobility, lack of expansion in cosmic realities, they are weighing down all that is and will be, just as when a human does not clear the tarnish and soot from within. When one human does not reach for the heights of his or her potential, he or she is then influencing the effectiveness of and, thus, the grandeur for all.

"Since bodies are vessels of transportation, they require maintenance. Joints desire lubrication, water requires cleaning and refreshing, bones, organs, and the full pulse of the vessel require nourishment for strength and durability. The whole requires detoxification from pollutants and contaminants that build up. All components of the soul's totality require attention for optimum stability in creating maximum duration. Interestingly, we are already witnessing examples of this lesson reaching humans. The increase in healthier eating, exercise, mindful actions, and higher consciousness are entering our screens of observance. The studies indicate easier absorption of this lesson than initially expected. Despite the attention,

heaviness still runs rampant in many humans. Since the tone
is double-pronged, we anxiously await filtration of the
balance of the truth message. Let me ask you this, Student,
do you not feel the heaviness when you are with the human
realm?"

"Yes, Teacher, your information is ringing a truth
within me. I feel many humans carry heaviness within them.
They are not clear and buoyant, receptive and uncluttered;
rather they are dull and despondent and some even feel
stagnantly unhappy."

"Much of the despondency you feel, Student, is the
lesson that you have been taught before regarding humans
having fallen off their purpose for entering the life they are
currently leading. This misalignment with their truths breeds
much of the black growth of heaviness within them because
of the dis-ease of unfulfilled purpose. There is an
additional therapy for this stagnation that will alter the
depth of infiltration, thus alleviating the weight the
permeation creates. Though aligning with one's truths and
purpose is the exemplary cure, there is a healing technique
utilized for reducing the expansion of the negatively
charged energies that encapsulate such joyless emotion.

"This healing lesson teaches the importance of tone management and has to do with tones that are submitted and the utilization of the correct tones. Everything and everyone emits a tone. These tones join the universe and all the submitted tones dance together to create a widespread collective tone. The stabilizing of menacing tones is vital for balancing the health of the Oneness of the universe. Tones ring in different octaves. These tones are not audible to every human, but they do register with the soul because the soul has memory and reacts to the memory of pitch. The scale of tones goes from shrill tones that create a sense of urgency and chaos down to tones that are deep and dismal provoking feelings of the same. As with everything, balance is fundamental and quintessential. Creating an awareness of these tones and aiding with the leveling of undesired octaves will support the healing of all, to benefit the healing of One."

"Teacher, how do we permeate this message through humans when they cannot hear the tones and thus do not know of the importance?"

"All souls know of the registering tones and consequently their importance. I taught that. Since everything is connected and One, the combined tone from all creates the One tone. When there are frequencies that interfere with the tone of Divinely blessed expansion, those occurrences need to be corrected, bringing the out-of-balance higher and lower frequencies to the level steadiness of Divine growth. Some humans radiate in such high-pitched tones that they affect all they are around by creating chaos, distraction, a sense of flighty, erratic pandemonium. Maintaining this high- pitched frequency requires much energy; and to maintain their tone, these humans will drain the energy of those they are around. Most are unaware that they are emitting reverberations that are detrimental to themselves, to others and, thus, to Oneness. They appear to be highly energetic and always dynamically driven. This comes at a cost to those who are giving their energy to these humans because they are drained of their own energy just so the high-pitched human can maintain such shrill heights. Helping these humans to ground their energy and tones will aid in the erratic fluctuations known to accompany such behavior as well.

On the opposite spectrum, some humans wallow in low tones that induce a sense of lethargic pessimism and a lack of enthusiasm. These humans have a tendency to look for the unpleasantness in situations and remain floundering in that vibration, wondering why they feel depressed. Around other humans, they are known to bring a blanket of despair and gloom to the group. These humans' tones register too low on the scale; and once adjusted, they experience balance in reactions, philosophy, and enthusiasm.

Just as the tones of singing bowls help balance and calm, so too can a human body's tones calm others. When we aid in adjusting the out-of-sync human tones, the pitch that a subject rings will cavort in complimentary fashion for the universe. Is this information comprehensible, Student?"

"Yes, teacher, I can feel the lesson as truth. Helping human souls to ring with the purity of the Divine tones will not only be advantageous in the human realm but in all realms and in all things and in the Oneness that is. Will the humans that are realigned with their tone remain in the correct pitch?"

"We teach lessons with the pure intention that those lessons be understood and endorsed and implemented by the beneficiary. The recipient, human, in this case, learns the lesson and even begins to perform in a new way, indicating a grasp of materials and approval based on actions. Then, unfortunately some receivers of lessons regress to old patterns of behavior as though they had never been enlightened with a higher awareness. This is a difficult process to watch, since we know the benefits of staying in the plane of higher learnedness. Not all recipients of gifted lessons regress, but more do than is desired. We are hoping this current shift in higher consciousness in the human realm will allow the transfusion of lessons to remain as valued information that is no longer deprogrammed, unappreciated, or dismissed. Because of free will, we cannot force humans to accept something or do something, even though we see the benefits far outweigh not taking an action. We *can* maintain the full Faith that our continued efforts and strides at infiltrating areas that once had no assistance will create a domino effect in advancements and positive propulsion."

Chapter Nine

The Lesson of Omnipresence

"Beautiful Soul, we will now practice dividing ourselves between assignments. You have learned how to work in different Now's and with multiple assistance. Now you will work with dividing of yourself for different assignments. This is your lesson on omnipresence. You will need to be present with your full senses. Open yourself to all the information and it will automatically come to you. Your being knows what it needs to do and how to do it. Trust this and allow it to happen. This is true in any case and in any realm. Being omnipresent simply means being ever-present within yourself, within others, within wherever you put your intention. You will have the ability to help more than one human at the same time. We all have the ability of ubiquitous, with thought and intention, to separate our focus onto more than one place instantly and unlimitedly."

"Yes, Teacher, but I have confusion about that which you speak, omnipresence. I am concerned that I will be unable to perform at the required pace, not being equipped with the tools of this technique."

"Come, Beautiful Soul, we have an assignment that will utilize our omnipresent abilities. By feeling this lesson performed, you will comprehend how it is positioned and then completed."

"Jake[13], it's your turn."
"My turn for what, you old goat?"

[13] Cross refer to real-life Angel stories 13a and 13b

"Your turn to go get us another drink," Sam hollered back. "Bring the bottles this time; save us a trip later." Jake begrudgingly walked down the flight of motel stairs that led from the rooftop pool to his motel room. The other five stayed behind laughing and finishing off their drinks. They had enjoyed a great day at the World's Fair, a trip they had planned since the location had been announced. The three couples had shared numerous enjoyable occasions, whether it was traveling or just staying home in their small town. One thing was a constant, no matter where they were, there was always plenty of partying and today was no different from the rest. They woke early that day in an effort to beat the record crowds that were anticipated and to get a jump on the temperature that was forecasted to soar in the high 90s. Walking around on pavement and concrete in a thicket of people would make the anticipated 90-degree temperatures feel much more like temperatures in the 100s. The couples knew they had the pool and cocktails to return to, which would help cool them off as well.

The roof-top pool connected two motels. They stayed in the motel to the east side of the pool. On the west side stayed a family also partaking of the activities the World Fair had to offer. Like the adult group, the family had sights on the pool as a great source of relief after a day of crowds and heat.

Jake returned to the pool where his friends anxiously held out their glasses. The air was filled with laughing and stories, each filled with an ample amount of profanities. As the family, consisting of a mom, dad, and two girls, made it to the top of the stairs with the pool in view, the parents were immediately taken back by the adult scene they were now privy to. The girls were half way to the pool throwing down their towels along their course, when the mom called them back. Not wanting to hear their mother, they continued a couple more steps before heeding. The parents decided that the atmosphere was not one suitable for their daughters to witness, so opted to return to the pool later that evening. Every step the daughters made after receiving the news was intentionally heavy, just short of a stomp, as they all made their way back down the stairs to their room. The adults in the pool had not even noticed the family's entrance and nearly immediate departure; they were too busy immersed in their own pleasures.

As promised, after a few hours and much pleading, the girls, accompanied by their father, rushed back up the stairs, giddy about who would make the biggest splash. As the three came to the summit of the stairs, the father was disappointed to find the adults still in attendance. Though the hours had passed slowly for the girls, they had not for the adults were still engulfed in heavy alcohol consumption. At this point, their mannerisms and slurred speech demonstrated that point.

The father, not wanting to disappoint his daughters again, decided he would let them swim for a short time as he closely watched them. The youngest daughter was three quarters of the way to the shallow end of the pool, which was farthest away from their entrance by the time the older daughter and father made it to the deep end. Three of the adults were yelling and laughing in a corner of water at the deep end, but then walked away toward the shallow end as the father and his daughter approached them. Confused at the adults' actions, the father looked at the corner that had initially captured the adults' attention. At the bottom of the pool was a man, face down and slumped over, nearly resting on the bottom of the pool, his arms hanging loosely. He was one of the men belonging to the adult group. The father grew quite concerned and turned to the group of adults who were still laughing and, of course, drinking. "How long has he been down there?" he directed his question to the group. Because they did not hear him the first time, the father repeated his question in a much louder tone.

"He is just faking it," answered back one of the adults.

"How long has he been down there," asked the father again, this time in a very loud, authoritative

Page 237

manner that was hard to ignore. His actions gained the attention of the group, who stopped talking. "He is just trying to fake us out," answered Jake, though his answer was a little uncertain. Obviously he was trying to recall just how long the man had been in the water. With that the father directed his oldest daughter to jump in the pool and to pull the man, who was still lingering at the bottom of the deep end, to the surface where he could pull the man from the pool. The daughter obliged, immediately jumping in, swimming down to the bottom of the pool and grabbing the man's motionless arm. The girl struggled fiercely to swim while pulling the limp body behind her, finally making it to the surface and to her father's outreached hand. The father pulled the heavy, lifeless body out of the water and onto the concrete by the pool. The man was unresponsive. The father had learned CPR when he was young. He hoped he had retained the needed information. He turned the man on his stomach, put his head to the side and cleared his mouth. Next he instructed his daughter to put her hands under the man's face to prevent injury from the cement as he applied CPR to the man. By this time the younger daughter had joined her father and sister and watched with astonishment. The adults had also gathered around, shocked at what was taking place before them, stammering and stuttering their alarmed disbelief. The father pushed hard on the man's back, then grabbed the man's upper arms and pulled them up. Over and over the father pushed and pulled. The victim's body lay motionless. The father continued, pushing harder on the back, pulling the man's arms back further to open the airway. Finally the man began sputtering and water spurted from his mouth.

A moment later the man moved his head, then immediately reacted to his position in a fighting manner. He pushed away the hands that held his head from injury and rolled his torso to release himself from the hold that had him pinned to the ground. The father fell. The man pulled himself to his knees and then in a wobbly manner lifted himself to his feet, wildly swinging his arms at anything that was within his reach.

The younger daughter screamed in fear, turned, and ran as fast as her legs could carry her to the stairs that lead to the safety of their motel room. The father and older daughter withdrew from the reaches of the man, who was still swinging and now yelling through his expelling water. His friends gathered round him and called his name, trying to make him realize where he was, what had happened. The father and daughter left the roof and moved down the stairs and back to their motel room. When they opened the door to the room, the younger daughter sat on the bed next to her mother, crying. The mothers face was white with fear of the unknown. Her wide-eyed stare met theirs as they entered the room. The daughter was crying too hard to make a full sentence, thus the mother did not know what had happened. Once inside, the story was told and they were all consoled. They were not able to go swimming that day, but they had been able to do something that not every person has the opportunity to do- they were able to save a life.

"Beautiful soul, you did well working your omnipresence with this assignment. You needed to aid multiple humans, with multiple missions. Giving the young girl the persistent, unwavering desire to go to the pool that evening and supporting her with the parental approval of such a yearning. Helping the older girl to have strength beyond her belief and to be fearless, so she could maneuver the heavy man to her father's waiting hand. To help the father recall his life-saving teachings, so that he could bring life back to the perishing man. Allowing the man to receive enough air in his passages so that he could take a breath again. Teaching all the adults, as well as the children, how fragile a life is and how relentless pursuit of a toxin that is known to cause harm, can do just that—cause harm.

Learning to work your omnipresent ability has been one of the last lessons that I will teach you."

"Thank you, Teacher. The sensation of dividing myself between different humans and aiding them simultaneously with their roles in an event was a daunting thought at first; but once I put intention behind my desires, it flowed easily."

"That is why I tell you, Beautiful Soul, to never allow your thinking to overshadow your abilities and truths. Over-thinking situations distracts one from allowing natural senses to perform at the optimum level. Always engage all that you have available to you, not just the thinking portion, but all your senses."

The[14] workload was heavy that day, no time for breaks, and the lunches were cut short. Her stomach growled as she helped one customer after another, most in less than congenial moods, complaining about their wait times, not realizing, I am sure, the conditions the employees were operating under that day. Maggie thought to herself, as she forced a smile to her face while watching the last such customer walk away from her

[14] Cross refer to real-life Angel stories 14a and 14b.

desk, sometimes it is easy to be so wrapped up in *self* that one forgets others are human with their own set of adversities. She made a mental note to always remember to extent hospitable interaction to every contact she made. Many lessons can be learned by being observant enough to receive them as such.

"Come Beautiful Soul, we are needed immediately. Our assignment is varied and we will both need to utilize our omnipresent abilities." Without responding She prepared herself for the shift between realms, closely shadowing her teacher's lead. "I will need you to be present with your full senses on this assignment. Open yourself to all the channels you need, receive the messages that you need to accomplish our mission, and assist all those that we need to help. I will feel you and you will feel me, we will work independently but together; and, between us, we will orchestrate the required tasks."

Many miles away, a long line of customers stood before Maggie's husband, his face blank as he stared at the computer screen. Behind him, the pacing manager glared his direction and with a huff shook her head, allowing anyone who was in the vicinity to witness her annoyed behavior. The man continued to stare at the computer, his blank expression changed reacting to the behavior of his manager. Feeling pressure, he pushed a few keys on the keyboard hoping it would trigger a memory for him, hoping it would remind him why he was standing in front of the computer in the first place. It did not. His direct supervisor, prodded on by the manager, approached him. "Doug, is there a problem? Those people have been waiting for a long time for you," He looked at her, but was unable to reply.

"What is it? What is your problem?" the manager joined them. Observing his actions, she reached out and grabbed the paperwork from his hands, "Here, watch out, I will just do this for you," she again huffed, exhaling louder this time, glancing at his supervisor, again shaking her head. The man stepped aside.

"Are you feeling all right, Doug, do you need to go sit down for a bit?" his supervisor queried.

He nodded his head, the best he could do, then mustered, "Yes, I think I should, I do not feel well." He went to the break room and sat with his head in his hands. He was scared. What was happening to him? Why could he not think? Why could he not remember what he was doing or supposed to do? He did not feel well. He could not determine what didn't feel well; he just felt *off*. Being extremely conscientious about his work ethic and performance, he gathered himself to his feet and went back to work, still feeling dazed and confused. His supervisor and the manager were very concerned with the flow of customer service, all things he was concerned with on a regular basis; but today was not a regular day. As hard as he tried to keep pace with his work, he was unable. For some reason his thoughts did not come to him, as though they were blocked before making it all the way. Noticing he was still having difficulty, his supervisor suggested that he go home, perhaps make a doctor's appointment, and get some rest. Before leaving work he phoned his wife to let her know that he wasn't feeling well and was going to leave work and drive to the doctor's. Being overly consumed with work herself, she asked that he keep her posted with the prognosis. Arriving at the doctor's office, Doug found a waiting line, but after explaining his symptoms he was shown right in. The doctor examined him thoroughly and before making a preliminary diagnosis excused himself from the room. He went to call the hospital to see who was on staff that afternoon. After determining and speaking to the doctor on call and explaining the patient's symptoms, he returned to his patient.

"Sir, it is my opinion that you have suffered a stroke, but we will not know for certain until you have further tests. I have already spoken to the doctor on call at the hospital and have told him of my findings and that you would be heading that direction now. Who drove you here?"

"I drove myself here. I left work and drove here directly," Doug replied.

"Your work let you drive yourself?" the doctor asked in amazement.

"Yes," was all Doug could release, being consumed with the news he had just received.

"You need to call someone to drive you, do you have someone close by?"

"No, not close by. I can drive myself, I drove here."

Doug made it to the hospital where he was immediately admitted. He requested one thing, to call his wife, Maggie, as he had promised to keep her updated. The news was received as anyone would expect, with utter shock. Maggie hurriedly hung up the phone after assuring him she was on her way. Despite her heavy workload, there was nothing more pressing at the time than her husband. Driving the long, forty-five minute route to the hospital was arduous. She called her brother. No answer. Then she dialed her sister. Again no answer. They both lived over two hours away. Her hands were sweating on the wheel, her heart pounded, her throat filled, and she could barely swallow. Tears streamed down her face as she drove, panicked at the thought of what she would find, feeling lonelier than she had ever felt in her life, alone, racing down the road to the hospital where her husband lay. A young man, healthy, suffering a stroke, how could this possibly happen? she thought to herself. Who can I call? Who can help me? Then the answer became crystal clear. Maggie called on the one thing she knew would always help; she called on God. She began praying and prayed the balance of the drive to the hospital. Once at the hospital, she ran in, asked directions, and quickly made it to her husband's room. His face lit up when he saw her. Maggie took his hand and greeted him with a question, "Where is the doctor?"

Almost as though summoned, the doctor walked into the room. She asked Doug a series of questions, examined him, and then asked him to demonstrate his motor skills. One of the requests was to stand and walk. Doug obliged all her requests, the last walking across the room. She stepped back, her brows furrowed, tilted her head, looked at the patient, then excused herself from the room. Doug and Maggie sat nervously waiting, unsure why the doctor had excused herself without an indication why or a report, even a partial report, on his condition. If allowed, a person's mind can run rampant with possibilities, searching for answers to questions that permeate the mind, unfortunately most leading to negative outcomes.

The doctor walked back in the room. "I am sorry I left so abruptly, I needed to examine your file again. You see, I thought perhaps I had the wrong file or the wrong patient because your symptoms did not match your x-rays."

The couple sat stoically, unsure of what the doctor was referring to.

"The x-ray that was taken of you, Doug, shows severe damage to your brain. When we see damage at this magnitude, there are always noticeable symptoms like paralyzed limbs or face, affliction of a certain side of the body, or even whole body paralysis. You answered all my questions, walked around the room, and performed as though the x-ray images of your brain were not yours. I have never seen a case study like this before. Now, we still have concern because you have bleeding on the brain. We will have to closely monitor you to determine whether you will need brain surgery, but your motor skills are amazing."

The next day brought equally miraculous news. There was no sign of bleeding; it had vanished. The doctors warned Doug and Maggie that there could be a high probability for another stroke, and the next stroke would be much worse, possibly even fatal—horrendous news to hear as one is being checked out of the hospital and sent home. Doug was surrounded by the love of his family, extended family, and friends. Prayers were made and answered. Time passed and threat of imminent strokes passed as well.

"Beautiful Soul, we have watched while the family's awareness of the matrix of assistance rose. They now know that life is filled with surprises and can change in a micro-second, but one thing is always there, always constant: there is always help, whether it be the help of friends and family or the help from heaven. Help can come in unexpected ways and from unexpected sources. Support may not always come exactly as asked for it; but when humans ask God and the Angels for assistance, it will come in the best way suited for the purposes of the lives of those involved. They have only to reach up and ask.

"We have done well with this assignment. It was not time for this human; he has much to do, many ways to serve the purpose of his path. He has many people to touch with his story of pure Faith despite the obstacles that were attempting to negatively afflict him. We needed to provide instantaneous healing from his emotional attack."

"His emotional attack, Teacher? Is that what caused his condition?"

"Humans who carry around a lot of hatred and negative energy can inflict pain and harm on other humans, knowingly and unknowingly. They spill pessimism and disapproval on those they are around, stabbing their victims with emotional wounds that fester until they become physical wounds. That is why it is imperative that we help the human realm feel the joy of Divine light, help them to remember Source and the unconditional love found there, and remind them to always shine their best light on others. The more they do, the more that bright light will grow within them as well.

We did competently, helping all the humans around this man to see that good shines brighter than bad. You helped the man's wife as well, something you inherently sensed. Protecting her on her drive as she rushed to be by his side, you wrapped your wings around her vehicle and created a Bluelight of safe passage to her destination. You wrapped your wings tightly around her heart to provide support and protection. You placed your right finger to her temple and reminded her that she was not alone and to call on our help. You also provided safe and clear passage for the family members, so they could be by the man's side. Plus, you granted one human visions and messages in her recharging hours, 'movies in her eyes,' so she could see and hear where attention best be spent. You showed this woman that the injured human was safe from harm's way now, but another human of connected energy to these humans was in need of attention."

"I was unsuccessful with that endeavor teacher. The woman did not see what I was showing her. She did not see that her attention needed to be on a different family member, that her mission was elsewhere."

"You were not unsuccessful, Beautiful Soul. That human will realize the lesson you taught her. Sometimes humans do not immediately recognize the sight we share with them. It takes practice for them to have Faith in what they are seeing or what they are hearing because they have shut down so much of their own abilities for receiving messages. We must continue to share these tools and lessons with the human realm in hopes that in doing so it will trigger the truths and memories that they hold deep within them. Just as we have aided this family with the sight of pure love and Faith, so will they share the knowledge with all they touch. The light of Divine shines brightly in them and they are not afraid to shine it for others now. Knowing that all will receive it as they are intended to, when they are intended to."

Page 250

"You have done well with learning and utilizing your omnipresence, Beautiful Soul. Some omnipresent assignments will entail you not only performing different duties simultaneously but will also necessitate a part of you staying on with the assignment for longer durations. You needn't be concerned with this. You operate at full performance with each element and realm that you are in, even though a portion of you remains elsewhere. That is the Divine beauty of our abilities: we never become drained by dividing off sections of ourselves for different purposes. All realms have this ability; however, some realms have forgotten it, as is the case with much of the human realm. Humans can operate different tasks simultaneously, not only in their realm, but in other realms. Various humans recognize this and have competency with it, but many do not. Some humans allow multi-tasking to drain them of their needed energy for life instead of calling on us for help and connecting to the flexes of limitless support and energy geared for Divine purpose. They attempt to do it all on their own. It is our strong desire to help humans become better humans. In doing so, as you have learned, we are increasing the positive charge and awareness level universally. We want to help them achieve their purposes and truth of being for their lifetimes, but they need to remember to ask for help. We all work together for greater good. We are all to help one another. Just as the rain waters the roots of the tree and the tree in appreciation drops nuts for the humans and animals, such is the duty of all beings: to work in unison for the greatest good of all.

Your next assignment will allow you the opportunity to practice the skill of dividing omnipresent competence and it will award you the occasion of feeling this division. As I said, it will not harm you and it will not take away from any assignment that you undertake concurrently. It will allow you the fortune of helping more than one assignment at a time, creating a mastery of Divine support."

"I look forward to helping many assignments synchronously, Teacher. What bigger blessing could one bestow upon the universe than to give as much and as often as possible?"

"You are correct, Beautiful Soul. You will attend this assignment alone. Remember, you may always call upon us for help. Open yourself to receive the knowledge that is within you. Have Faith without doubt, knowing that you have all that you need and you are fully supported by all that is."

She readied herself for the familiar transitional shift between realms, anticipating what would await her, what the assignment would entail, who she would be helping, how she would use her omnipresent abilities as her teacher indicated.

The woman, releasing tears of pain that had been bolted down deep within her for years, curled up in the fetal position in her bed. She was surprised by this feeling of deep anguish that embodied her still. She thought she was well beyond the grieving period. This sudden outbreak was unexpected and unwelcome. She hated the feeling of being miserable and out of control, of having feelings that were difficult to climb up from and that funneled downward into depths of sorrow, like a tornado hitting the ground spewing debris and destruction everywhere it touched and leaving behind it a path built of sadness that would necessitate mending and renovation. Perhaps that is what she needed, to be completely revamped like an old home that has been overhauled and refurbished with loving care. That thought made her body twinge. Instantly the pressure of gloom and despondency that had her clutched within its vortex released, as though she had been defibrillated with paddles of joy and excitement. She inhaled new air, deep into her every cell and essence. She stretched her once aching body out and sat up in bed, half expecting to see an actual light bulb floating above her head because the inspiration came to her so suddenly, with so much impact. The idea excited her. Not just excited her, thrilled her. It filled her with a breath of positive air, pushing out all the old toxic air that she had been encased in so quickly that she could not feel its gravity any longer. Swinging her legs over the side of the bed and standing up, she could not move fast enough. She had not been this excited about anything in more years that she could immediately recall. Out of shear wonderment at receiving the idea, as well as feeling the way she now did, she looked up to the sky smiling and said, "Thank you."

The clock on the bedside table in the little motel room where she was staying read 1:30. Not too late at all she thought gleefully with an inexplicable sense of urgency. After pulling on a pair of jeans and slipping on a sweatshirt, she grabbed her keys and purse, then opened the door of the motel room that she had called home since her husband passed away. The fresh air rushed passed her, the scent of the flowers impregnated her sense more deeply than she remembered ever having experienced before. The sunlight caressed her with warmth and made her eyes squint briefly as she

Page 254

adjusted to it. More than calling this motel home, she had used it as a barricade to shield herself from the taxes of her life. She was enthralled with a new found sense of the grandeur of life. Locking the door behind her, she was off on her adventure, an adventure that sparked life back to a once comatose existence. It was time that she found a new home, a new life; it was time that she started living again, giving back to life again, and allowing life to give back to her. She permitted herself to be immersed in the faith that she was being directed on a path. It was not the norm for Gabrielle to allow anyone or anything to control her, not that she was a control freak; she just liked being in control and having a readily accessible outcome because of it. Today changed all that. She sat in her car driving in directions that the road signs pointed her, completely unaware of where she was going and not completely sure of why, but not allowing any doubt to damper her new found faith in life. As she rambled around the back-country roads, her senses were completely open granting her the opportunity to absorb all the beautiful sights and smells, as though it was the first time she had witnessed the picturesque displays nature has to offer.

She began to feel a bit confused with direction, never having traveled this far away from the sanctuary of her motel room. As though on demand, just ahead appeared a gas station. She opted to stop in for some help. The kind gentleman was more than helpful and pointed her back to the road that lead to where she had asked to go- at least she thought so. Forty minutes later, houses began to appear and then grew closer together, an indication that a town was approaching. Off to the right was a large wooden sign, that appeared to have been hand carved and painted announcing the upcoming town of Bowmont.

When Gabrielle read the name of the town, her heart danced, which inspired goose bumps to frolic all over her body, putting a smile on her face. Her smile must have been quite obvious because as she drove into the town, she was greeted with waves by two separate individuals out walking their dogs. A friendly town, she made a mental note. The town consisted of a main street and several side streets, most of which were lined with residences, not businesses. It was not a large town in any way; but there was something unexplainable about it, something that made it feel familiar and comfortable to her as though she had arrived home and, once there, she didn't want to leave. She found herself donning a permanent smile as she explored the quaint town, driving slowly, peeking in the storefront windows like a child peeking for Santa, attempting to catch a glimpse at what lay inside.

Each visit she made to Bowmont proved to be longer as she familiarized herself with some of the businesses, stopping in for lunch at the neighborhood diner that seemed quite popular with the locals. Her explorations led her on back roads that saddled spreads of land so vast it was not easy to identify size. Picturesque ranches pastured cattle and horses; some even cradled llamas and alpacas. The lure of the area was inescapable. Soon she was purchasing a home, just as the notion had befallen her that day not long ago, a home that required renovation, just as her life did.

The home's revamping provided multifaceted benefits. Not only did it endow her with a much needed soul cleansing, it afforded her the opportunity to be part of something again. When Gabrielle purchased the home, she had visions on just one project, a house renovation. In actuality, she was renovating her life, removing the old, worn, unneeded entities and replacing them with new, happy, vital things. She achieved a sense of purpose from all. Along with the metamorphosis transpiring within her and the home, she had the opportunity to become involved with people again, to be part of a community and a new set of friends, good, salt-of-the-earth people with complex paths, personalities, and life experiences.

One such meeting was with an elderly woman, who owned an antique-curio store in town. Their relationship blossomed immediately and proved to be a deeper soul relationship than any she had ever experienced. Hours were spent together sitting in the little shop, while Violet schooled Gabrielle on the towns' people, as well as many incredible stories from her heterogeneous past. The experiences that this elderly woman shared were all consuming. It was difficult for Gabrielle to believe at times that all the stories were coming from one person's life, these vast far-reaching stories that spanned the globe, touching romantic eras and desperate times, each bringing with it a story of fortitude and grandeur. It truly was hard to believe that such a small, frail woman had so many experiences in just one life. Days turned into months as their relationship spawned new life in Gabrielle.

"Beautiful soul, you know that it is nearly time to conclude this assignment. We know your ties are strong with this human and you can see much goodness in her as we can. There are times that assignments end without further commitment, and there are times when assignments end gradually with evident documentation. We are allowing you to finalize this assignment anyway you feel will best help this human and all the humans involved in this assignment."

"Thank you, Teacher. I feel quite woven into the fiber of this particular human. It gives me a sense of sadness thinking my time with her must come to an end. I know that it must. I know that she will never fully dedicate herself to the mission statement she entered her life to accomplish if I do not provide for her the final lessons of Faith."

"Yes, you are correct, Beautiful Soul. You are all that is good and kind of Divine making. You are pure love. We trust that you will handle this assignment just as you have handled the others you have orchestrated."

Chapter Ten

The Lesson of Multifarious Participation

and

Physical Manifestation

"Beautiful Soul, we must work quickly. We will work concurrently with many others on this assignment. Beautiful Soul, we must leave now. There are many of us assisting with this assignment and you will feel their diverse energies around you.

Each is tasked with their own portion of this assignment. Numerous humans are involved and in danger. Stay close to me. We will all split up when we get close and aid in various ways with this assignment. The human realm does not realize yet what is to happen."

"I am concerned teacher. I have not heard this tone in your voice before, such a sense of foreboding and urgency."

"Stay aware and close, Beautiful Soul; open your senses. Sense all that is. We all need to work independently and in conjunction now."

She stayed within the familiar energy of her teachers as the whirl of magnetic energy encased them and began shifting them to the human realm. Just before they were aware in the human realm, she felt a division of energies, as though a mass separation were occurring. Energies were jetted away from her in a circular pattern. She felt alone, but then recognized her teacher was still with her. It was just the two of them. "Where have all the others gone, teacher? We all began the shift of realms together, but then it was as though there were a flash and all the energies separated and went in all directions."

Page 262

"As I mentioned, Beautiful Soul, many of us were appointed to this assignment; but because of the size of this mission, we all have our own segment to be accountable for. What you felt was the separation of energies prior to fully interlocking in the human realm, each moving off to aid its delegated sector, just as we have. Bring your senses back to front; be present in this Now."

"Where are we, Teacher? I have not been here before, but it is familiar to me. I know what this is. I have felt this movement before. There are many people. Who is our subject?"

"Yes, Beautiful Soul, this is a mode of transportation that you utilized when you were in the human realm. The humans have entitled it a train. It moves many humans from destination to destination. There will be times when our assignment involves multiple humans at one time, such as all the humans on this train. Several of the energies that split from us before we entered the human realm are assigned clusters of humans on this assignment. We will help one. It is not her time, so we will help her avoid certain peril. Do you see the woman with the dark, curly hair? She travels alone. Her energy is strong and determined, yet still curious for her life's adventures. We need to open her senses so that she can hear and see her messages. Though she is very advanced in attunement, she has not learned to listen, see, and feel all that is good and not good for her. It is time for her to open more, so that she can hear her higher conscious, her higher-self, and so that her higher-self can protect her."

"How do we broaden humans' capability to recognize and trust themselves? These are traits that all humans have within them, their own truths; this you have taught me, Teacher. So, how do we remind them of themselves? Remind them of the importance of trusting the messages that they send to themselves and those of Divine making?"

"In this case, Beautiful Soul, we must open this woman's senses now so that she will not doubt the messages that she is sending to herself. Once we trigger a truth inside of this human and allow the messages to immerse into her being, then it will be difficult for her to ignore the importance. The human will feel the nagging sensation at every junction, physically, mentally, emotionally, and spiritually. Her body will react to the messages she sends herself, her mind will be consumed, her emotions will heighten and it will be difficult for her to ignore the repetitive

Page 264

communication. That awakening is what we are to help this women with."

"Will she always remain open to her own messages from this point forward, Teacher? Once we help her hear herself, when she understands that she is sending herself the truth, will she always trust her messages?"

"Unfortunately, Beautiful Soul, many humans will regress and will not maintain the heighten awareness to trust themselves, to listen to themselves without doubt. It may take a couple of our involvements with a human before they will remember that trust is a gift they can give to themselves. Trusting their inner messages and truths is not only a right they own but a natural protection clause that is interlaced within each being."

"Will *this* human remember to utilize all of her senses without doubt or fear after our involvement with her today, Teacher?"

"That is something that we do not know. We can reach through realms and veils and shed light, open memories, awaken hidden truths and raise conscious thinking patterns, but we cannot control humans. They have the free will to make choices that affect them, other humans, and the world. All that we can do, Beautiful Soul, is be with them to aid and protect, shine them with pure love and light, and pray that they will remember all the Divinely brilliant characteristics that are woven into the matrix of their soul and being— all the principles and assets that they participated in composing for themselves. Our time is Now."

She watched as her teacher moved to their new assignment. The woman's body was bouncing in unison with the bumps and turns as the train maneuvered along the tracks. The teacher moved her hand toward the woman's head, toward the woman's temple, and then placed her pointer finger against the woman's left temple. She saw a spark of white light. The woman jerked and looked to her side, finding nothing. She rubbed her temple. Her expression changed. Her brows furrowed and her lips tensed. Her mind was filling. Her eyes narrowed as she looked out the window. Her mind filled more, filled with the messages that she was sending herself, the senses of foreboding, unease and anxiety. As the train clanged along, the woman absorbed more of her own messages. As the train slowed and then came to a stop, the woman rose and disembarked.

Using[15] her full might, she pushed the last of her clothes into her backpack readying for the final leg of her trip before returning to college in the fall. Cynthia was a seasoned traveler, often taking off on her own to explore cities, even countries, much to the dismay and unease of her parents. Her current travel, which had taken her through Europe to a month in Istanbul, would continue with then a stopover in Athens before a tentatively planned meeting with a friend in Paris and then a return to Stockholm for school. Her parents were relieved that she was finally exiting Turkey. The country had been in unrest for some time, no place for a young girl, they insisted.

Hefting her backpack onto her back she winced, surprised at how sore she still was after having carried the bag around for over a month already. The muscles should have been conditioned by now she thought. Though she had only picked up two new shirts and one book, her bag felt taxingly heavier as the weight, coupled with gravity, tugged on her sore shoulders. No time to complain she thought to herself, knowing that she was running late already. The train to Athens would depart soon and she needed to be on the train to make it to the airport for a flight to Paris to meet her friend.

[15] Cross refer to real-life Angel story 15.

Though they had not confirmed their meeting for over a month, Cynthia did not want to do a no-show to a prior commitment, especially with a friend, though something inside of her was hesitant about the trip.

Not a moment too soon, Cynthia made it to the train station, jumped on the train and secured a seat. Her shoulders throbbed from the weight of her backpack. The bouncing of the train on the rails almost felt therapeutic. She closed her eyes in an attempt to catch a nap before arriving at the airport. Her mind was too busy to sleep. Cynthia first thought of the amazing experiences she had in Turkey; then she thought of Paris and wondered if her friend would actually be there; then she thought of school and the classes that she would need to take. But underneath each thought, an uneasy feeling was brewing. Something in this intensified feeling made her abandon thoughts of Paris. She searched in her mind for reasons for the increased urgency of the message to change her plans, but she could find no concrete reason. The one thing she did know—she could not go to Paris; she needed to get off the train. Listening to her plaguing inner voice, she obeyed and disembarked at Athens and spent the last of her vacation days exploring an island in Greece, far away from the media. Only when she reached Stockholm, did she learn that her planned flight to Paris had been hijacked and many of its passengers murdered.

"Our project is complete here. Our assignment is safe."

"Beautiful Soul, you have another assignment.[16] You will be equipped to help this case because you will be able to feel what needs to be done."

"Yes, Teacher, I shall do as you request." She felt herself prepare for the shift and readily accepted the tingling sensation associated with it. She found herself in the midst of beautifully fragrant flowers. The colors and smells were so compelling and captivating that She wanted to absorb all that She could. The floral aromas, coupled with the scent of freshly cut lawn, permeated the air and her senses and triggered memories of times gone by, of her lives gone by in the human realm. She remembered these earthly bouquets and, as She recognized them, they were like perfumes for the soul, evoking joy and filling her full of natural earthly energy. She sensed the woman before her filled herself with the same natural energy when she was around these realms. The woman and She were in a place

[16] Cross refer to real-life Angel story 16.

where the woman could go and feel happy and at peace. The Earth realm, Nature realm, and Fairies realm were all present with the woman.

The woman was not aware of how much these different realms came to her when she was with them watering the flowers, enjoying their beauty, smelling their beauty. It was as though these realms danced with happiness when this woman was with them, happy because this woman appreciated all the effort that it took to create such beauty when they knew many humans did not show such respect and gratitude for the works of art created by these realms. Most humans do not see the flowers shaken by the fairies so that they will be noticed and smelled to their fullest potential. This woman saw the beauty of a flower; she allowed her senses to fill with the beauty that was intended for the human realm to enjoy. This woman did not yet realize that she was not alone when she was in her garden; she only knew that it was a place of beauty, a place that made her feel good and happy and took away any stress that might have clung to her during the day.

It was just that reason that lured her to her sacred garden that day, the stress of a human life experience that is often taken as a casualty. The woman stood in her chapel, nourishing the very things that nourished her in return.

She watched as the woman unknowingly interacted with things she did not see. She felt the heaviness of the woman's energy. The woman was filled with much sadness and fear. A cloud of forlornness hung over her; tears rolled down her checks. She watched as the realms worked with fullest might to cheer the woman, to bring her the joy that she often felt while with them in this sacred spot, but their efforts were to no avail. She heard the woman's unspoken words, pleading words to God and the Angels asking for help. She felt this woman's words come directly to her. She had received the assignment from God to show this woman that her prayers had been heard and that all a human has to do is ask for help and then the Angels can step in and help. They cannot help without an invitation. Not all prayers will be answered exactly as they are asked, but they will be heard and answered to the greatest benefit of the humans who are involved and in alignment with all their life purposes at the time.

She heard this woman's prayers. She felt this woman's fears and anguish. She raised herself in the sky and expanded the energy around her. With intention She created herself as brilliant sparkling jets of golden light in a blanket of Angel dust. She hovered in front of the woman long enough for the woman to fully see the radiance of the display. The woman watched the gleaming, luminescent cloud of light, at first with uncertainty, confused by the presentation. She didn't know what she was seeing, if it was real or a reflection off something, perhaps the water she was using in her garden. The woman moved the direction of water's spray; the effervescent display continued, more vibrantly than before. The woman dropped the hose to her side and stared at the unearthly brilliance in front of her.

She felt the woman realize the communication that was being shown to her. She saw the woman smile. She felt the energy of the woman shift, as though the heavy darkness that she was encapsulated in was dropping off, a section at a time, as though an egg were being peeled of its shell. The woman stood tall and began glowing.

She drew near to the woman and wrapped the woman with her wings, cradling her softly and gently so that she could feel full, pure love from the Creator. She pulled away from the woman but left a blanket of the pure love around her, a blanket that would shelter her and protect her from the harms the woman had once feared. She touched the woman's temple and a jet of Divine light entered the woman, light that would awaken in the woman the truths of her being, the truths of her strengths in desires and goals, the strengths that were her truths for overcoming obstacles. She gave the woman a permanent wave of recognition of self, so the woman would have peace and not fear or doubt the infinite possibilities of determination when directed by pure love.

The woman nearly stumbled in reaction to all the information that she just witnessed and received knowingly and unknowingly. Yet, the woman was at peace. She wanted to scream to the world that she had just witnessed a miracle. She wanted to cry because she was so humbled by the visitation. The woman did neither, she picked up the hose and continued watering her sacred space, this time smiling and radiating from the Divine intervention that bestowed upon her a wealth of information that would make itself fully known throughout the years ahead.

He[17] slammed the cupboard door closed as a direct reaction to Kathy's words. "I thought I told you I

---

[17] Cross refer to real-life Angel story 17.

didn't want to go with you tonight. I am sick of you controlling everything I do and say. Can't I ever get any peace around here? Just leave me alone," he yelled over his shoulder with venom as he stomped out of the room, picking up his keys as he was leaving. She could feel her shoulders curling in, her posture slumping as though she were coiling in on herself, trying to cover her hurting heart, attempting to protect it from yet another painful stabbing. She could hear his car engine start and then the tires as they squealed their way out of the driveway and down the road. Tears pooled in her eyes.

Behind her she heard the innocent voice of her youngest son, "Isn't dad going to watch my concert tonight, Mommy?"

Kathy quickly wiped her eyes in a manner she hoped would not to be recognized as such. Turning, she looked down on two big brown eyes staring up at her. She could feel her heart twisting inside her chest at the thought of her untarnished child suffering at the hands of a man that was not able to share of himself at this time.

"Dad has to work late tonight honey. He just left to go in." Though she did not like lying to anyone and knew that she was not being honest with her child, she felt it was better for him to hear this rendition of the story, rather than sharing the truth. "We will still have a lot of fun tonight, and I am very excited to watch you!"

Her answer seemed to satisfy her son, though nothing would completely take the place of having both parents supportively in attendance. She kneeled down and wrapped her arms around her son, applying a huge hug and multiple kisses, which created an "ooh-yuck" reaction, which always made her laugh. The grief and anxiety that her husband created was counterbalanced by the love that she shared with her sons. Her elder son was quite aware of the increasing conflicts within his parents' relationship. He was also quite aware of the decreasing time his father spent at home. He often made a point to acknowledge this to his mother as a form of support for her. The three, mother and boys, were blessed with a very close relationship, no doubt the result of the examples taught to her in her youth by her own mother, nana, and great auntie. The close ties Kathy had with the women continued until each left her life on earth to ascend to her next steps. She was especially close to her auntie, whom she had spent much time with, since her own mother was sickly. Her auntie was a minister who that graced her with the truths of Creator. Since her auntie had no children of her own, she lavished her niece with unconditional love, as though she were her own daughter. Her nana also bestowed upon her wisdom of another kind, administered with pure love as well. Their influence gave her the strength to recognize truth and good through the troughs of hardship and betrayal.

As if having a faltering marriage were not difficult enough on a person, her beloved business, to which she had given so much of herself, was also faltering. The pressure of life overtook her at times, and she would withdraw in private and release as best she could the sadness that lingered and grew more and more within her.

Sometimes when one is not paying attention, a hand reaches down and helps a person realign with purpose, though at the time, it is unclear that that is what has happened. Such was the case with this woman. Feeling completely deflated and unable to carry on, she reached for her great auntie's bible, which she kept on a shelf at her workplace. Often times holding the bible tightly to her chest would make her feel more peaceful, as though her auntie was still with her. As Kathy pulled it off the shelf, a piece of paper gently floated to the floor. Puzzled, she picked it up, unfolded it, and read it.

There, on the worn sheet of white paper that had been under her great auntie's bible was a note scripted in her mother's handwriting; it was a prayer, not just any prayer, but a prayer just for her, just *to* her. Her hands trembled slightly realizing what she was seeing. She was instantly flushed with a sense of well-being, as though she were protected and not alone. It reinforced the nucleus of her very being. She felt her shoulders stiffen, elevate, and move back; she felt her posture straighten; and she felt stronger and more alive than she had in years. She was completely enveloped with a sense of purpose and the knowingness that she would be fine. she was not alone. Her mom, her nana, and her great auntie were with her and would be with her whenever she needed them. Kathy and her sons had the strength and unwavering support of a source much greater than any visible source. She looked up to the sky and smiled. She was overcome with pure love and Faith. She thanked all that were with her then and thanked all that would help her always.

"Instilling the sense of connectivity to source is a valuable lesson that you have learned well, Beautiful Soul. I knew you would recognize it when it was time to come to the aid of this woman again, and you did without prompting. Humans carry such pain and sadness within them that they need not carry. It is part of our purpose to help teach them that it is not necessary and certainly not good for them or for the energy circuit that they are providing to others and the universe. With each lesson we share with the human realm, we are helping raise this vibration circuit to one that is lighter, more positive, and more transcendent. I recognize

Page 277

you feel and believe this now, Beautiful Soul. You were also able to call on the help of departed loved ones on behalf of this woman's sake. They willingly administered much needed love to her essence and supplied a physical example of their never-ending presence in her life. That example re-charged the woman, so that she will have the Faith to remember these things without prompting in the future and so that she will help others with these truths as well. That is Mastery level."

"Thank you, Teacher. Yes, I can feel the goodness that this woman has within her, and I can feel how she had lost sight of it, lost sight of herself. She had allowed others to steal from her the goodness that she was known for, that she was made of, thus leaving her an empty shell that she no longer recognized. Her departed loved ones were saddened by her lost lust for life and her blindness to her own Divine value and image, so they readily contributed tools to trigger hidden memories, tools that would enable her to see the truths of her being in this life. It is quite satisfying to help humans see their own reflection again, so they can shine that reflection on the world."

"Yes, Beautiful Soul, it is a sense of Divine goodness and purpose that we are blessed to awaken in the human realm."

The fire [18]cracked and roared as J.B. threw on another log. Throughout the campground other campers were doing just the same, building fires that would warm and entertain them throughout the evening hours. The smoke bellowed up through the tall fir trees and lingered just below the top of the tree line, making a slightly eerie sight from a distance.

Krystal was busily preparing the items that would comprise their dinner at the end of another beautiful day. She loved coming to this campground. Nature always seemed to relax her, as though just being part of it drew out all her cares and worries and sent them soaring to the sky with the smoke. The children loved it too. Rules were much more lax, and they were allowed to run and play and get dirty. The campground also had many other children for them to play with. New best friends were made on every trip. The lake provided a perfect swimming hole, a place to cool off and rinse the dust off as well. The corded-off swimming

---

[18] Cross refer to real-life Angel story 18.

section delivered a safety net for swimmers and allowed parents to feel more secure as their children splashed and screamed much of the day away. The family had enjoyed coming to this campground many times. Each liked it for their own reasons. J.B. enjoyed rising early, hiking around the side of the lake with his son, and throwing a line in the water. Most times they did not bring home anything but tangled lines and "almost" stories; occasionally they would bring home a trout or two, which were praised and applauded and then cooked in a fry pan over the fire for breakfast. Krystal not only enjoyed the relaxation that she so cherished, but she was also awarded a reprieve from a sense of the constant parenting and entertaining role that most parents are quite familiar with. In nature there is much to occupy everyone, once they discover how to look. They also learned that taking some activities camping was a wise decision as well: cards, board games, bikes, and of course no camping trip would be complete without Smore's.

Krystal looked up with a smile as she heard the laughter coming from her two children. "One last ride around the campground; then it will be time to wash up for dinner," she hollered. This announcement was met with dismay, as the children had endless energy it seemed. Krystal watched as her son, Ryan, maneuvered his bike in and out of campsites, effectively hitting every pothole, which prompted a shrill screech from her daughter, who was positioned on the back of the banana seat.

"Mom, can we go around one more time, please, please. . ." They both yelled back almost in unison.

"All right, just one more time, but then no more," Krystal almost laughed back her answer, quite familiar with the," just one more" request.

"Yippee, I am going to go really fast this time," Ryan shouted as he hit another pot hole. "Let's go the long way around this time," he hollered over his shoulder, making a turn in the direction of the main road.

"No, no. . .slow down," came the response from his sister, Judy, in a half-laugh. Then in a panicked voice she hollered, "Stop! Stop now!"

Her brother's foot came off the pedal unsure of what his sister was reacting to. "What, Judy?"

"Stop! I saw something in my mind." At that she leapt off the bike and rolled to a stop in the dirt at the side of the road.

Her brother, nearly crashing head first because of her exodus, managed to skid and slide sideways to a stop a couple of feet from her, almost at the edge of an intersection.

Just then a large Winnebago RV sped past them. They both sat stunned. Finally Judy was able to speak. . ."I saw that RV coming."

"How could you see it coming? The trees were there. I didn't see anything," retorted Ryan.

"I saw it in my mind. I saw the RV coming and we were just entering the intersection. I cannot explain it. . .I just had a picture of us and the RV and I knew that we had to stop before we were hit," reported Judy in a wobbly, uncertain voice.

Shaking and in a state of disbelief, they walked the bike back to the campground and relayed the story to their parents.

"Beautiful Soul, you have instinctively done well again. This was a difficult task, showing humans pictures in their minds to save them a fate that was not theirs to have.

This will be the last time I will join you on an assignment Beautiful Soul. You have proven that you are capable of handling many different assignments and you have Divine pure love and compassion to manage them at the highest level. It has been my pleasure and an honor to work with you."

"I do not feel that I am ready to work without you. I think I still need your help."

"Remember Beautiful Soul, to *feel*. When you feel, you are using your soul to search for answers and make decisions. When one thinks too much, then the truth and answers become restricted, clouded, and based on a process of elimination instead of expansion. When we feel, we are expanding ourselves to accept all the truths and answers that the universe can bequeath us. Then we are utilizing the full expansion of learning—mind, body and soul. So you say "you think" that you are not ready; but you see, Beautiful Soul, you just limited yourself. Instead always remember to feel. In this case, you will feel that you have all that you need for every assignment that you are given.

Feel, Beautiful Soul, and the universal truths and answers will be awarded to you."

Chapter Eleven

The Lesson of Physical Intervention and Multifaceted Skills

She felt the familiar stir of energy that occurs before an assignment appears in her mind. As the communication made itself clear to her, she recognized the importance and urgency. She enveloped herself with the sheath of energy required to move from realm to realm. All the skills that in the beginning had seemed difficult came readily to her now. She could, with ease, move from realm to realm, use all senses for the receiving and delivering of messages. Though she had always had a natural ability to see the solution and complete an assignment regardless the nature, the solutions seemed to meld into her being even more quickly now, nearly simultaneously with her obtaining each project. This time was no exception; She would be using varied techniques that She had been taught to ensure success. She had a vision of the victorious outcome. Teacher had taught her how to multiply her vibration and magnify it into a mass recognizable in the human realm. Teacher had also taught her how to change her own tone to a tone which was audible to humans. These were advanced teachings in preparation for an assignment such as the one that She had just been given. These and her own instincts would all be needed Now.

The night [19] air chilled Mailey as she jumped into her car, eager to get to school for practice that started at 7:00; she glanced at her watch, only 6:45, plenty of time, no need to rush. She turned on the ignition and let it idle

---

[19] Cross refer to real-life Angel story 19.

for a few minutes to warm the engine before pulling out of the driveway. The steering wheel felt ice cold, which forced an uncontrollable shiver through her from her head to her toes, so she shoved her hands in her pockets to warm them while she waited. Glancing in the kitchen window, she noticed her mom was looking out, watching her. Mailey gave a swift wave through the window and her mom happily returned the gesture. The exhaust puffed warm clouds of vapor against the cold night air. Excited to see her friends and nervous at the same time that she would not remember her new part, she put the car in gear and pulled out on the main road headed to school.

The radio exploded with one of her favorite songs, so she reached over to turn the volume up higher. Singing along with all vocal chords fully engaged, she marveled at how much she sounded like the artist. Tapping her hand on the steering wheel to help the percussion, she motored down the road toward practice. As she reached over to turn down the volume on the radio in accordance with her enjoyment of the new tune, she inadvertently knocked her notebook off the console next to her. With her left hand on the wheel and peeking over the steering wheel she reached down to gather the fallen article, just briefly removing her eyes from the road. When she returned her focus to the road, she was shocked that in that minute amount of time, her vehicle had entered the oncoming lane.

She grabbed the steering wheel with both hands and jerked it to the right, back to her side of the road; however her enthusiasm in doing so was too great and she overcorrected the direction of her route. Her car leapt off the side of the road, plummeting down the embankment. Plowing through dirt and rocks like a sled on ice, her car jetted down the steep hill toward a field. A boulder caught the left front wheel catapulting the car forward and onto its roof. Skating out onto the field, the car slide on its roof for what seemed like hours, over mounds, screeching and thumping along its trail, thrusting through a barb wire fence, and finally coming to a stop, all four wheels still turning.

Dazed, she knew she needed to exit the vehicle, having watched TV shows where cars burst into flames after crashing. Although Mailey was stunned by the events of the last couple of moments and was hanging upside down with her head nearly touching the top of the car roof, she worked hard at gathering her senses. Reaching over, she felt for the window handle so she could roll down her window, the same window through which she had waved goodbye to her mother just minutes earlier. Every move was a struggle because of her position; but she managed to roll the window open. Feeling for the opening, she tried pulling herself through the window, but could not move. Almost panicked she tried again, harder this time. Then she remembered she had not released her seat belt. Slowly Mailey felt for the buckle and unfastened the belt. Instantly, gravity slammed her down onto the roof of the car, where she landed in a rumbled ball. She forced herself to stay focused and again reached for the window. Though her mind danced around all that had happened, was happening, and could happen, she pulled herself through the window, out of the car to safety.

Though shaky, she could not feel any major injuries and was engulfed by an unexplainable calm, despite the circumstances. The night was exceptionally dark. There were no street lights on the remote country road and she could barely see the correct direction. The stench in the air was nearly nauseating, a combination of tire rubber, earth, metal, and engine oil. Feeling the ground in front of her as she moved away from the car, she found the barb wire fence that her car at sheared moments earlier. Carefully negotiating her way forward so she would not get caught in the barbs and separating the wires as she progressed, she crawled through. She looked back and saw she was safely away from her vehicle now, from any possible fire or explosion, she thought. She sat down on the mist-covered grass and pulled her cell phone from her pocket. For the first time,

Mailey noticed that her hand was shaking slightly, though she still did not feel scared. She called her mother, "Mom, I have had an accident." A call and words that a parent hopes never to get. When she hung up the phone, she heard a voice from the distance.

"Dear, dear, are you there? Are you all right, dear? Can you make it here to the road?" The voice came strong and clear through the chill of air. It had a familiar tone to it, like her grandmother's voice; but Mailey knew it was not her grandmother.

"Yes, I am all right; I am out of the car."

"Come this way, dear, follow my voice."

Mailey made her way through the field to the embankment by the road, following the directions of the elderly voice. She slipped and slid her way up the embankment, over the loose gravel, rocks, and mud, making it to the side of the road. There stood an elderly woman with white hair tied securely on top of her head in a bun. The elderly woman reached her hand out. She took it.

"Oh my dear, are you sure you are all right? That was a terrible accident. Did you call someone? Do you have someone coming to help you?"

"Yes, I phoned my mom, she told me that she would come immediately."

"Oh good, dear. Just relax now; everything is fine. It is all over and you are safe. You have nothing more to be worried about." The elderly woman held her hand tightly and patted her back in a loving gesture with her other hand. It did make her feel warm and much safer and calmer with the company.

Mailey could see headlights approaching her and thought to herself, please let it be my mom. The elderly woman broke her thought, "Here comes your mom now. Everything is fine; you are safe." Mailey recognized the headlights; they were from her mom's car.

"Wave your arms, dear, so that your mother can see you standing here. Wave them high."

Mailey started waving her arms in the air as high as she could make them, almost wanting to jump up in an effort to be seen. The car came to a stop in front of her. Her mother leapt from behind the wheel crying, "Oh my Goodness, are you all right? Are you hurt?" Her mother's expression was panicked.

Her brother, equally alarmed, jumped from the passenger side of the car, running to his sister's side, eyeing her up and down for signs of injury.

"No, I am actually okay."

"Where is your car?"

"It is down there," and she pointed down the embankment toward the field. This information triggered another reaction from her mother, who was still wrapping her head around the fact that her daughter had been in an accident alone in the dark.

"Your car is down there? You drove off the road and your car landed down there?" Her mother asked, half-traumatized at the idea and fighting back the sobs. "How did you know where to walk? How did you find the road? It is so dark," her mother questioned her while applying the necessary hugs and kisses.

"This woman helped me." Mailey turned to her side to point at the woman. There was no one there. She turned around looking for the kind woman but could not find her. "Hello, are you there? Where did you go? I want you to meet my mom and brother. I want to thank you." There was no answer. The night was silent.

"When did you say she helped you?"

"She guided me to the road with her voice and stood with me until you got here. She is a very kind, elderly woman."

Her brother, now reacting to this information, tilted his head in a puzzled manner. "There was no one standing with you when we drove up, Sis. You were standing here alone."

"Don't be silly, she was right here. She told me to wave my arms to you so that you could see us."

Her mother hollered, "Hello, I want to thank you for caring for my daughter. Are you still here?" There was no answer. The elderly woman was nowhere to be found.

"Mom, did you see anyone standing with Sis?"

"No, I didn't."

"I only saw you, Sis. No one was with you."

The three stood and stared at each other as truth bumps ran up and down their bodies.

Upon demand She was present in her next assignment.[20] She was in a home, in the garage of the home. It was dark. She sensed something wrong with the large metal human transportation unit. There was a problem with the vehicle, a problem that could create catastrophic results if not corrected. She sensed the humans moving toward the garage and then to the auto, taking their places in the automobile and turning it on. It was a woman and a man. There was no time; she instinctively created a long piece of metal and shoved it deep into the rear tire on the passenger side. The woman backed the car out of the garage, and the couple drove off without noticing the nail in the tire. She stayed with the humans and the automobile. She waved her hand over the tire again, summonsing a loud knocking noise

---

[20] Cross refer to real-life Angel story 20.

from the tire. The woman heard the reverberation and slowed, listening closely. She requested the man to listen for a noise. He heard nothing. They continued to drive. She waved her hand over the tire again, initiating an increase in the volume of the clank.

The woman heard the intensity level of the hammering sound increase as she drove and again slowed down, focusing on the origination and location of the noise—the back passenger tire. The man heard the sound. They pulled the car over and the man got out to examine the tires. He found nothing because the skies were still dark. The man had to fly out early that morning to his work. Time was of the essence; so having found nothing, they continued on toward the airport.

She responded wrapping her wings around the humans and the vehicle. She created a beautiful Bluelight that wrapped the vehicle, and She created a tunnel of Bluelight that projected from the front of the vehicle toward their destination. She held them tightly as they made their trip to the airport. Then, again projecting a Bluelight in front of the vehicle, She held the woman and

Page 294

the automobile in her wings as the woman drove back home in the beautiful protective Bluelight. When the sky lightened, She kept her wings wrapped around the unit, as the son, after finding the nail, carefully drove the affected automobile to the closest tire center. She released the vehicle and the human knowing that they were safe.

She then felt the familiar swirl of energy that came to her just before she was given an assignment. She loved the Angelic help that she was able to provide to so many in the human realm and was always excited to see what the next assignment would entail. Without fail, the steward passed the new assignment to her. This was to be no small feat. She would have to utilize all her skills and then some to orchestrate this one. Filling herself with the glittery mist and full essence of Divine She shifted realms moving into the human realm. She placed herself in a bedroom of a home. In the bed lay a young pregnant woman feeling her first contractions of labor. She called upon the earth realm for unified assistance and then She called upon ascended relatives, a grandmother and grandfather of the woman, to lend encouragement and support.

The young [21]woman was scared and alone. Tears rolled down her face, tears representing a multitude of emotions. Tears of joy for soon she would be blessed with a beautiful child, tears of fear that the delivery would be more painful than she could bear, tears of anxiety that her child would be unhealthy, tears because a terrible storm had covered the city and surrounding areas with snow and ice, which made travel difficult at best. This beautiful young mother lay alone, fearing that was where she would stay, alone, unable to make it to the hospital, unable to have family with her during this joyous event.

She reached a finger to the side of the woman's temple and gently touched her, igniting a spark of purple light. The woman did not notice; she was deep in concentration. She then raised her left arm in the direction of the Heavens, palm up and placed her right hand on the mother's stomach.

---

[21] Cross refer to real-life Angel story 21.

The mother opened her eyes and looked around to find no one. Unsure of what she had felt, she closed her eyes again and wept.

A golden, spun filament of light streamed down from above, piercing through the roof and ceiling material. She looked up to her Creator and smiled. The Divine filament flowed down her left arm, through her, and down her right arm and palm that was still placed on the mother's stomach. Then it entered the mother's abdomen into the child resting peacefully in the mother's uterus.

The mother again opened her eyes, feeling warmth on her stomach; for a second time, no one was there. A peace came over the mother, a serenity that was unexplained.

There was a knock on her door, then familiar voices. It was her family; they made it. They were with her. As they packed for her and moved her carefully to the vehicle to drive her to the hospital, the woman continued to feel warmth permeating throughout. When the young mother arrived at the hospital she was greeted with smiles and gladness, which helped vaporize her fears. With family at hand, she delivered a beautiful healthy baby girl.

When the Golden Soul entered her new life, as though on command, the clouds parted and the sun's warm rays jetted through, touching the earth and melting the ice, brightening the skies with golden-yellow exhilaration. The heavens sang because on this day a beautiful little girl entered the world, a beautiful golden soul with her own Truth of Being and her own purpose path that would help all of human-kind.

Chapter Twelve

The Lesson of Ascension

They[22] were seated in chairs facing the doctor's desk as they waited for the doctor to return. His desk was messy with stacks of files and papers, two laptops and a tablet. There were three pictures sitting on the credenza behind his desk, one of a woman posing with a

---

[22] Cross refer to real-life Angel story 22.

tennis racket, one of three children on the beach making sand castles, and the last, a formal shot of the whole family. They were a beautiful family and all looked happy and healthy. The walls were adorned with plaques announcing various credentials and with four framed photos of animals like those found in Africa; a giraffe reaching for a leaf high in a tree, a herd of elephants running across the barren plain kicking up a huge dust cloud around them, a herd of zebras calmly eating, and a flock of birds taking flight above a brown body of water. The photos were nicely matted and framed, as though the photos held great significance. The man and woman fidgeted in their chairs, glanced at one another with a smile, but remained nervously silent, ready for the doctor.

The doctor walked back in the room after gathering the remainder of the test results. This time his expression had changed. He was no longer smiling and walking with an upbeat stride; now his shoulders were slumped, his mouth was drawn, and he avoided eye contact. The reading of the report was not necessary. They could tell by his demeanor that it was not good news. Joyce fought back tears and sniffed quietly. Tom put his hand on her leg in a comforting manner.

As expected, the news from the doctor was not good and, unfortunately, it was worse than either of the two were prepared to hear. They both bravely attempted to fight off the devastating information that was overtaking them as the doctor read the news. Once in the car, they felt comfortable allowing the bottled-up emotions to flow out. Joyce was finally able to cry and sobbed into a napkin she found tucked in the pocket of the car door. Tom sat stoically, though all color had drained from his face. He robotically maneuvered the car out of the parking lot and to their home. News of the prognosis came equally hard for all of the family. Tom was a good father, grandfather, and a kind loving man whom few did not immediately like.

The doctor was accurate in his assessment of the ravages of the disease and the anticipated timeline for Tom. He lasted just a few months after being told of his illness, and they were long agonizing months for everyone. Watching someone melt away in excruciating pain is almost unbearable, especially someone who is so deeply loved.

After his passing, family and friends mourned his loss and kept him in their hearts. There were so many unanswered questions—things that should have been discussed, but were not—a mistake many families make. When you know the end is close, it is time to talk about anything and everything. It is uncomfortable, but you will not have the chance later. It is not worth living with the regret, based on the safety of silence.

In addition to things that could have been discussed with Tom, after his departure another unvoiced concern, the largest concern for many of Tom's family, was where he was after passing. Each member thought about it, but no one talked about it as though it was off limits, wrong, or inappropriate. So, in the back of their minds, they all wondered not just about Tom's location after ascension but also about everyone's ascension. Was he okay, did he make it to Heaven?

She watched as the family tearfully threw flowers on the casket. The adults hung their heads wrenching in pain from their loss. The young children knew it was a sad time, judging from the examples the adults were providing, but they could not yet grasp the eternal commitment that a loss of life is. She knew that there were unanswered questions, concerns about ascension. She could feel the questions, but they went unspoken between the humans. She felt the compelling need to provide information to these humans, information that they could take forward and share with others, information that would help other families who have difficulty talking about matters of death, passing, and ascension. Touch one human with knowledge and you touch all that they touch. She knew this family needed her help; they needed to know, so others would know. She felt the time was not right. She would have to wait. She would feel when they were ready to hear the message that needed to be delivered.

She let two weeks pass after Tom had been freed of his human vessel and allowed to join God and the Angels. The two weeks saw some healing with the families grief, but still there were concerns and unanswered questions. A loved one may pass on to another realm, another purpose, but they are never lost. There is not a black hole that extracts all that depart from a life, never to live on in eternity. She needed to help this family know this truth. She needed them to feel this truth, so they would share this truth.

She received many assignments now and many assignments she could perform simultaneously since Angels are omnipresent. All She had to do was will a directive and it would be completed. She could will many directions concurrently and they would all be accomplished. She placed herself in the bedrooms of two of Tom's grandchildren. They were beautiful Golden -Souled girls and both were sleeping soundly. She could feel and see their Divine glow; She could see the important purposes that these young humans had for this life. She was warmed being in their presence. Children carry the beauty and innocence of Divine with them until they are taught otherwise. She entered their subconscious dream state and prepared a vision for them. It was a vision of their grandfather happy and healthy. He was playing with them and laughing; they were all laughing. He had no pain. He glowed with joy. She helped the children to feel the joy that he currently was feeling, being freed of his tired, sick body and being able to learn lessons and prepare for his next purpose destination. She helped the children saturate this knowledge so they would remember it in their waking hours.

She knew that the message to this family had to be received by more than just the children. She shape-shifted herself into a human figure of a man and positioned herself in the human realm at a table of a restaurant that was frequented by one of the family members. She sat and waited. When She knew the time was close, She reached through the veil and asked Tom to assist her with the last part of the assignment. Tom melded into her and became the likeness of the man at the table, becoming one with him and She becoming one with Tom.

The family member walked through the restaurant focused on nothing but a meal until she reached the table. With a glance, the family member's eyes were held by the eyes that looked back at her. The woman stopped abruptly in astonished recognition when their eyes met. The man stared back at her and smiled a warm familiar smile. The family member kept walking but wanted so badly to take another look, another look at the eyes that she knew, the eyes she had looked into for so many years, the eyes that looked back at her so lovingly for all the years. The family member knew what she had seen, who she had seen.

She touched the temple of the family member to trigger the memories that she had stored within her. Instantaneously the family member knew that she had just seen Tom and that Tom had delivered a message to her that he was fine, that there was a somewhere after death, and that a person was never lost, just somewhere else. The family member knew that Tom was still around. She helped the family member understand that communication is not impossible with those that have ascended; it is simply different from what we are familiar with in the human realm. The more the belief of eternal life is internalized, the truth of it becoming part of the reawaken truths of the universe, the easier communication between realms will be.

His body ached,[23] a deep ache as though every inch of him had been pulverized, just as the hay had been earlier that day when he rode his sturdy John Deere tractor through the fields pulling the loud machine that cut the hay and placed it in rows to dry. His eyes and sinuses still burned. Though he suffered terribly with allergies and hay fever, the job had to be done. When the crops were ready, there was no waiting. It was not like a vacation that could be put on hold or grocery shopping when one could make do with what they had, sometimes indefinitely. Crops were more similar to a test. It will be given to you at a particular time and you have a predetermined span to finish it. If you are not punctual, attend to it in the correct timeframe, and complete it prior to expiration, then it will affect your grade. The grade in harvest being the quality of your product and, thus, the usability of it and the price the harvest will reap.

So, despite his agonizing physical reaction to haying, the harsh pounding his body took when cutting and baling hay, he had to do it and suffer with the consequences later. As he made his way to bed, slowly

[23] Cross refer to real-life Angel story 23.

lowering himself down, wincing with every move, he felt grateful that the cutting was complete, though the thought was followed immediately by the tormenting reality that it still needed to be baled, thrown on the flatbed, and stacked in the barn. Luckily, he had doubled his hay fever prescription, though, in actuality, it seemed to make only a slight difference. As he lay in the twilight hours prior to falling to sleep, he imagined how his great-grandfather managed. His great-grandfather had started the farm and had built and lived in the farm home where he and his family now lived. Machines were much more limited in those days, if machines were even available. What took a day or two to accomplish now would take a week or better then. Though his body throbbed from the physical tax the job entailed, he could only imagine what his great-grandfather, whom he had been named after, felt at the end of his day.

Thoughts became blurred as sleep consumed him; he needed as much as possible to heal his body before the next step of the harvest.

From the depths of sleep, he felt a cold chill run up and down his spine. Consciously pulling himself out of sleep, he felt someone with him, then a cold hand on his face. Thinking it was his wife or one of their children, he opened his eyes to scold them for waking him. It took a moment for his eyes to focus in the dimly lit room, where muted light was coming through the curtain. As his senses awakened too; he opened his eyes wider expecting to see a familiar image, but then he squinted his eyes, unsure of what he was looking at. It was not his wife or either of their young children; it was an unfamiliar shape. What *was* he looking at? Before him floated a translucent white object similar to a cloud — a transparent, wispy fog hovering right before him. He strained to look closer at the image, blinking his eyes to clear the sleep film. The object was gone. With the blink of his eye, as though he opened them in a different window of time, the entity was gone. He laid there watching, listening, thinking; what had he seen? Could it possibly be someone from another veil, from heaven, visiting me, he thought? He was not afraid, instead he felt peaceful and loved. His thoughts lulled him back to sleep, calmly, gently wrapping him in serenity.

The next morning he told his wife about the experience and since she had not witnessed it herself, it was difficult for her to comprehend the likelihood of such an occurrence. As occurs with many of us, the instance, visitation, whatever it was that he had encountered was put up on the shelf of his memory. Often the rush and hectic pace of day-to-day life takes the place of many past events. They are not lost, simply put up on one's memory shelf.

The next night was a night like any other; the hard work of the day made the bed a welcoming place. He bent over and gently kissed his children who were sleeping. He stood and watched as their small nostrils pulled in the air and observed as their chests lowered with the exhales. He was exhausted; but no matter how tired he was, there was nothing that made him feel more alive and happy than his children. He smiled at their small beautiful physiques, each clutching their favorite stuffed animal or doll. Pulling the blanket up around their chins, he tucked them in and thanked God for the miracles of his children.

He wondered if his own parents enjoyed this vision as much as he did. The beauty of a sleeping child exudes innocence and grace. His heart grew heavy and then began to ache. He had just lost his mother and the love he felt for her was undeniable and the pain he felt daily from her passing was all consuming. There was a void in him, a void that could only be filled with the love of a mother. She was so young, way too young to die. He still needed her. His children still needed her. A tear came to his eye and rolled down his check as he thought of his children growing up without a grandmother as wonderful as he knew his mother was. His silhouette shriveled with loneliness at the thought of a life without his mother.

He made his way to bed, where his wife lay deep in the clutches of sleep. Quietly he lowered himself into bed. The physical requests of the day left him weak and in need of the regeneration that sleep provides. His eyes still wept thinking of his beloved mother. Slowly sleep began whisking his sadness away. His body twitched and awakened him from the near-comatose place he was headed. Instantly he was saturated and overcome with a familiar feeling. There was someone with him, someone in the room. He opened his eyes. This time his eyes did not need to adjust as they had before. Before him floated a brilliant blue ball. The ball floated in the air and moved in a circular motion, emitting striking rays of blue light from it. He was stunned and lay motionless temporarily; then quietly he reached beside him and awakened his wife. She woke with a start. He soundlessly directed her vision to the ball. They both lay in bed watching this beautiful display of energetic blue light slowly spin in front of them for what felt like several minutes, eventually vanishing into nothing. The room grew dark. There was silence for a moment and then he said aloud, "Thank you, Mom, for visiting us and letting us know you are all right and that there is a God and a Heaven." His wife expressed her gratitude for the humbling visitation as well.

From that day forward, he would never doubt the existence of other realms. He would never doubt the possibility of visitations from departed loved ones, and he would never doubt that communication is possible through all veils.

She and her teacher smiled with infinite pleasure knowing that their involvement in these humans' lives allowed the chance to awaken within them the truths of what lies beyond the basic human sight and communication. Humans become so fixated on the basic five senses that they forget vast abilities they once knew.

"We have done well here. These humans have felt and, therefore, they will remember. They will share these experiences with others and in doing so will raise the consciousness level of those they touch. That is what we all must do, continue raising the consciousness levels and in doing so we will create broader thinking, less restrictions, and vaster achievements."

Beside the bed sat family members, most of whom exhibited withered stature and swollen bloodshot eyes. There were few tears left to cry as they had released buckets full over the preceding days. Now they shared stories of past life experiences, most triggering laughter, a testament in the form of memories, to the joyous contributions the ascending human had left them.

"What did she say? Are they going to make it" Susan questioned James, who had just finished a call.

"Yes, they will be here tonight. Hopefully Mom will be able to hold on long enough for them to see her," responded James.

"Mom is very strong. I know if she has anything to do with it at this point, she will make sure that everyone who wants to be with her will make it."

"I agree with you, Sis, but I am not sure if there is anything left to her, if she knows what is going on or if her mind has gone and it is just her body that is here. Mom has not acknowledged us now for a couple of days. It is just hard to know if she knows what is going on."

"I understand what you are saying. I just choose to believe that she can still hear what is going on and that she knows who is here and what is said, like when we talked about the hide-and-seek game we played when we were kids."

"I hope Mom doesn't die on Meg's birthday, which would be difficult on her every year ahead."

"Yes, you are right, James."

She shifted back into the room with the human who was being prepared for her ascension. Two days earlier, two Surveillance Angels had swept through the top right corner of the room checking on stature for ascension. Now She watched and smiled as the Finishing Angels hovered closely over the woman's motionless body. It is their job to detach all cords that are not intended to travel with the soul. They also are tasked with embedding the cords of memories, lessons, and experiences that are to remain with the soul to aid it in developing the mission statement for its next life. In addition, these hard-working Angels are assigned to removing lower and negative energy that is attached to the soul, so those energies will not move to the soul's future missions.

There are many steps of preparation for soul ascension and many levels of Angels that aid with the process, depending on the path of ascension chosen by the soul and on whether the soul has chosen to depart the human realm quickly or slowly. In this woman's case, she had been ill for many years with a disease that had stifled the life in her needed organs. This woman had chosen to move through the ascension process slowly, thus the full array of

Angelic assistance was present, visible for all who were of the knowingness to tune in and witness.

The door opened slowly, creating a soft breeze that swept through the room. Meg's face appeared in the opening, followed closely by her husband, Daniel's. Judith's face was red, matching her eyes. What was left of her mascara hovered below her lash line. "We are here. Has there been any change?" she whispered.

"There is no need to whisper, Sis. We think it is good that Mom hears that you are here. Happy Birthday!" James gave his sister a big hug, then one to Daniel.

"We are so glad you guys could make it. Happy Birthday, Meg!" Susan shared hugs with Meg and Daniel as well.

"What is the status? Has there been any change?"

"No, things are the same as they were when we last spoke. I know this timing has to be hard on you, Sis, seeing it is your birthday today."

Meg just shrugged her shoulders and took a place by her mother's bedside.

She welcomed the Timing Angels who entered the top right corner of the room. They smiled lovingly back, knowing each was there to aid a beautiful soul in its return home. The Timing Angels advised that the Alignment Angels would begin calling in those who would be greeting the ascending soul and would advise the Gloried Escort Angels to prepare for escort the following day, per the instructions of the ascending soul. The soul and the body began the transition process. This transition is the human soul's physical example of participation in the ascension.

The humans were given the time they needed to be together and send final wishes of goodbye to their beloved mother. As directed, the Ascension Angels followed the soul's directive and prepared the path, assembled departed loved ones to greet her, and escorted the beautiful soul home. It was a magnificently orchestrated event and done just as the soul had requested.

She knew instinctively that it is important for the human realm to remember that, when losing loved ones, they are not lost; they are moving on with the process of their lives to create another opportunity to grace another human life with their newly chosen purposes and to move on to a different realm to do whatever is that particular soul's chosen right. She felt how important it is for the grieving humans left behind to release the departed soul with blessings and gratitude. In doing so, they allow the soul to move on and they do not tether it to a life that is finished by the elected terms of that soul. This is an area where awareness and knowingness are beneficial; specifically knowing that a loved one whose physical body dies suddenly is still present to communicate with, say good bye to, and make peace with prior to complete ascension.

"You have another assignment, Beautiful Soul."

"Teacher, I have not sensed you for some time. It is so nice to feel you close to me again, to feel your loving radiance. It is interesting you are here to give me another assignment. I have completed many tasks on my own. Why are you here with me again? A new lesson?"

Her teacher infused her with the new assignment. She felt blissful warmth engulf her, a deeper ardor than she felt with normal assignments.

"You will help a new soul who is joining us from the human realm. She will need to learn the lessons as you did when you arrived. You will be the Teaching Angel for her now."

A sense of joyous serenity faceted through her. "I am honored to be chosen for this role, Teacher. I anxiously await the soul that will be joining us. I have thought of her often. I ask that I have the fortitude, abilities, and wisdom that you have bestowed upon me to pass along to this soul."

"Beautiful Soul, you are filled with Divine Grace and pure love. You will be the perfect teacher for this Angel-in-training. Never doubt, for when you have Faith you have everything."

"What about this soul's other teachers? Will she have many others? Will I be to her like you are to me, her main teacher?"

"Generally new souls meet with many teachers for lessons. I had the honor, Beautiful Soul, of working with you the most. The wisest thing to do in most situations is to let the teacher assignments play out as they are intended to be. When you do that, then you are allowing the true artistry of Divine to weave the fibers of Mastery into the tapestry of each soul."

Gradually she was gaining consciousness. She opened her eyes; everything was white, like she was encircled by steam. Where was she? She struggled to remember. Where had she been? What had happened? Try as she might, the memories evaded her. She was unable to piece together the turn of events. Think, think, she told herself. What happened? Where was I? Where am I? Why can't I remember anything? She put her head in her hands and shook it back and forth in an attempt to jar the memories lose. She lifted her head and began looking around; this time she was able to begin seeing her surroundings.

Why am I alone? Where is everyone? She tried calling out, but no words came from her mouth. She could not speak. She tried again to yell, nothing.

The billowing white air moved around her; then there was light, twinkling, sparkling light, all around her. She was light. She looked for her hands, but they were not there. She could no longer see a human shape, she only saw a mass of sparkling white light, radiating, almost pulsating light. She was glowing light. At that same time she felt complete happiness, complete peace, complete calm and acceptance—a complete sense of belonging. She could *feel* and everything she felt was gratifying and pleasurable.

Slowly the white foggy air dissipated; she looked beyond her own glowing image and was able to see other masses encircled in radiating, shimmering matter moving toward her. Now all around her she could see and feel.

"Hello, Dear One, I have been waiting for you. Take time to acclimate."

"Where am I? Who are you?"

"You know me, Dear One. Take your time; you will remember. We have known each other in a different realm. I am very happy to be with you again."

"How do you know me? I do not know you."

"Feel me, Dear One. Feel who I am. Use your senses to feel me."

She gasped, "I feel you. I remember something, but it is not clear. I feel that you are familiar to me, that I am happy to be with you. How do we know each other? Who do I call you? "

"You may call me, Teacher, or you may call me, Violet, Dear One."

The End

Ascension Witnessing and Notes from the Author

On an Angel's Wing of Ascension

Anyone who has lost a loved one knows the anguish of farewell and separation. Many times there are unanswered questions, such as what the next step is for their loved ones, what happens when they leave this life, when does it happen, why does it happen? The list is endless and specific to the person; however, there are some truths provided by the Angels that apply to every soul ascending. I participated in a group distance healing. Unfortunately, by the time the healing group was called to assist the person, the contracted ascension process had begun. I was actually able to tune in and watch this person's beautiful Finishing Angels hovering closely near their "charge," and "working" on the person. I saw these Divine Angels look up as they realized the love that was being sent to their charge via the group healing, and I could feel the immense gratitude for us for sending love and light.

In this same healing, I felt our friend who was receiving the healing tell me that she didn't feel anyone loved her. It made her terribly sad thinking that she was losing her life thinking that no one, not even her family, loved her. I remember showing her with my mind's eye all the love that was being sent to her at that moment, all the people who were thinking only of her and sending her pure love and light. I watched as her once colorless physique gained color. I sat in bed with her (remotely) and held her head and told her again about all the people sending her unconditional love at the time. She was so happy, and a sense of gratitude and completeness came over her.

Because this was a distance healing, all participants including the subject were located in different areas, cities, and states. After the healing, my husband, who was out of town as well, texted a couple of us, "That was intense, we all need to talk!" Three of us joined together on a conference call. Amazingly and without prompting all three of us recounted witnessing the intense sadness this person was feeling at the thought of not being loved. Each one of us had surrounded this person with our words and love and told her and shared with her the love that we were bringing to her. This was an incredible occurrence for all who were involved. We all felt the same things, saw the same things, even though we were states away from one another.

If you ever doubt that your words or prayers go unheard, you need never doubt again. I have seen it and felt it and I have watched the results of it as well.

On another occasion my good friend's brother had fallen ill. The doctors were fighting a losing battle attempting to figure out the cause of his illness and, thus, were unable to supply necessary treatment. My friend contacted me asking that we say prayers and send healing love. I began praying and asking God and the Angels to help and then I talked to her brother telepathically. I could see with my mind's eye that he was quite troubled. I asked him to share with me what was wrong, and he told me he was afraid of letting people down and of disappointing people. I told him that we all have free will and we all have our own truths and path. No one would ever be mad or disappointed with him for taking the path that he knew he was supposed to take. I assured him that God and the Angels were all with him and that they, too, supported a person's free will and purpose in this life.

God knows and blesses a person's
purpose and truths with
Unconditional Love
God believes in each person.
This is truth.

I have been blessed and have had the privilege of watching two amazing women in their ascension process. One was my beautiful mother-in-law, an Earth Angel, and the second was my beloved grandmother. I was able to watch all the Angels that make their presence known during the stages of ascension. They work their assignments with love and honor to prepare the ascension and then gently and magnificently lift the soul from the human body and float it up to the heavens completely encircled, cradled, and guarded by the Escort Angels and by thicker density wisps of images that I believe to be departed loved ones opting to help with the journey home. The departing souls and Angels radiate in a blaze of golden-white iridescent light and radiate with all pure love. I did not see or feel any sadness, negative energy, worry, or any of the emotions in the ascending soul like those left behind were carrying and feeling. It was a moment of beautiful, pure white, unconditional love by all, as though the whole group were smiling and happy and floating with purpose, leaving behind anything that might have been heavy, sad, dark, or questionable.

I have been blessed with examples of how souls give detailed directives of departure details. My mother-in-law waited to ascend until the last persons scheduled to arrive by her side did so. My mother waited until two days after my sister's birthday to ascend. My father waited until two days after my son's birthday to ascend. My grandmother waited for the day after my sister's birthday. My grandfather passed the day before my niece's birthday.

With both my mother-in-law's and with my father's ascensions, I have been blessed to be shown examples of how the persons preparing for ascension are still able to know who is with them and hear the conversations going on around them. My sister and I had the honor of sitting with my father in the hospital on the last night of his human life. We sat all night and recounted stories of our youth, laughing heavily at some, crying at others. There were times in certain stories when my father's breathing grew very quiet as he listened to the end of a story. We knew that he was listening to us—we felt him—and he showed us with his breathing.

I have been blessed with examples of how the departed loved ones and the Angels are waiting for the soul. My beloved paternal grandmother was a vivacious woman with many causes. She was very intelligent and graduated college with honors. She involved herself in many clubs and organizations geared to the betterment of people. Through her work with the literacy council, private tutoring, Job's Daughters, and the creation of reading programs (the list goes on and on), she was able to make many friends and touch many lives. My grandfather was equally dedicated to involvement and shared himself with many organizations and councils. My grandparents would swim most every day in the beautiful bay close to Kailua-Kona, where they lived. They met in college and separated only because of my grandfather's passing when he was eighty-one. My grandmother loved to make friends and socialize, and it makes me smile to this day thinking about her continuous dialogue. She was a delight to all those who could appreciate her good qualities and intentions. I loved her dearly and miss her!

One of her favorite things was playing bridge. Because of this love, she taught bridge classes and began writing a book on the strategies of bridge. Unfortunately, she began suffering health problems and lost her ability to speak. For the last four to five years of her life she carried a tablet and pen and wrote down all her conversations. Not being able to communicate via the voice was a big loss for her, but she did not let it stop her and she moved on almost seamlessly.

At the end of my grandmother's life, I sat next to her in her hospital bed. I held her hand and sent her love and all good happy memories. The nurse was a wonderfully kind woman and knew that my dear grandmother did not have much time left, so she tried to give me as much time alone with her as she could. I appreciated her very much for that. I watched my grandmother move through the transition and progression stages. The nurse did have to check occasionally though and on one of the checks, my grandmother, who had not moved in a day, opened her eyes, looked up in the direction of the sky, and began moving her mouth. Then muffled words came from a voice that had not been able to speak for years. This happened for just seconds, and then she closed her eyes and peacefully passed. I sat in complete astonishment. I was holding her hand and I could not even move my hand from hers. The nurse then told me that she was talking to her loved ones in heaven and that she had seen this happen before. I sit now with tears in my eyes as I remember this long forgotten experience. I am humbled at the glory that is gifted to us. My grandmother was taken on an Angel's Wing to be with her beloved husband and all the other loved ones who had passed before her.

On an Angel's Wing of Prayer

The following is an important practice to use when asking for help—whether it is help with goals, dreams, aspirations, finances, physical/health issues, anything that you are asking God and the Angels to help you with.

1. State your desire with full intention. Do not ask for something that you do not truly want. If you cannot feel the yearning from head to toe then rethink your true desire for the request. When you place full intention behind a request/prayer, then it will encompass your very being and you will feel, see, and know that you want it. Sit back, ground yourself, close your eyes, and connect yourself to God, Creator, Source, and the Angels. Then ask for their help in bringing you what you request. Have a picture in your mind of that request being placed on an Angel's Wing and floating

up to receive the attention that it needs to be answered.

Remember that not all requests are answered immediately. What you request is given to you when the time is right for you based on the information that aligns with your truths and purposes for that life.

2. Once you have asked the universe for help, do not take it back. You have given this special task to the highest power there is. If you were able to make your desire a reality for yourself, you would have done it already. As I have said in my other writings, do not give it, then take it back and mess with it, then ask for help and give it again, just to take it back a few days/weeks later and mess with it some more until the universe is so confused about what you are truly asking for that it sits back and waits for clear intention. Once you have placed your prayer on an Angel's Wing and watched it with your third eye float away from you to heaven, then leave it; you have done what you need to do. Thank God and the Angels in advance for their help in answering your prayer when it is the best timing for you.

Page 332

"What Would an Angel Say?"

Most people have heard or perhaps even have used the expression, "it dawned on me." When something "dawns" on us, it is like a light being turned on, the sun rising over the mountains in the morning spreading its beautiful rays across the land, waking the realms and welcoming a new day.

Dawn is light. Light is The Divine Angels. So when something "dawns" on us, we have just received a message from the Angels. So, from this day forward, when something "dawns on you," remember to thank the Angels!

There are many beautiful stories and books written by equally beautiful souls that remind us to always watch our words, to pay attention to the words that we say, because what we project we will receive back.

We know that we must speak with awareness of effect and we know that words carry a frequency. By paying close attention to our words, we will begin creating a shift in vibration around us. As we spread this vibration and awareness, we will be creating shifts in people around us.

Our choice Now is to integrate this important information into our everyday speech, that is, to have a continuous awareness of chosen words, to ask ourselves, "What would an Angel say"?

We are all tasked in this lifetime with sharing and spreading our light.
It is a beautifully important job!

Realm and Angel Glossary

Departments of the Angelic Realm

Ascension—This department aids with the coordination of the ascension process for souls.

Advancement—This department monitors when Angels are released on their own to do assignments.

Healing - This department aids in the healing, alleviating, and rectifying of situations that are not in alignment with the directives of the soul's life plans. Its purposes are carried out by Healing Angels.

Loss Prevention—This department monitors and corrects situations that would place a soul in ascension before its chosen time.

Life Review—This department meets with all ascended souls and shows them a film of their lives and how their actions both helped and negatively impacted other souls. From this movie, the souls are able to outline a new list of items to be accomplished in their next life and are able to determine the truths of their being for that life and determine at what point they will reenter and which realm they will reenter.

Monitoring – This department is in charge of monitoring human activity on paths, purpose, and truths similar to the Earth Angels' monitoring assignments. The department monitors all human souls' activities to ensure alignment with their chosen path. Its activities are carried out by Monitoring Angels, who are also responsible for applying the progress made by human souls to the universal grid of advancement.

Realm Coordination— This department is in charge of surveillance of all realms and creating a cooperative effort for universal support, sending additional Angels to realms that are experiencing a large shift in energies and frequencies. The department monitors progress in advancements and coordinates participation between realms.

Teaching – This department manages the teaching Angels. It delegates the lessons and determines which Angels are to teach which lessons to which souls.

Guardian Angels

These Angels guard and protect the soul from any harm. Humans have their own assigned Guides, Counsel, and Guardian Angels, as do we in the Angelic realm. Each of us has at least one or two main Guides that are assigned to us and that, of course, have access to all the realms' support and knowledge. This is something we give freely and with pure love to each other and to anyone who asks for our help. It makes us very happy to be of service and to help alleviate problems. That is why we would be joyous to have all humans call upon us for Divine help and direction.

Guardian Angels also guard the soul until they hand it off to the Ascension Angel committee. They then stay with the soul for a short period of time to ensure that ascension is imminent before going back to the Angelic Realm to be reassigned.

Ascension Angels

Quick Ascension

The process and the Angels involved in a quick ascension are the same as for a prolonged ascension, though holding patterns differ. The Ascension Angels work in unison to accomplish the same feats as in a prolonged ascension. Every soul has requests and requirements for their ascension that are pre-agreed to contracted determines of their life. Ascension Angels have copy of each contract that the soul has made for ascension and they reference the contract with both types of ascension. The quickly ascending soul still has requirements of giving time to each beloved human prior to complete ascension, so they hover just above the human realm allowing any humans left behind, who so desire, a chance to say goodbye. Some rising souls will elect to hover above the human realm if they feel a human soul that has not made their amends and released the departed soul to move on.

Prolonged Ascension

Surveillance Angels— These Angels often avoid detection, as they move in and out of radius quickly, typically using their sense of attunement to the assignment to judge the disposition. They are large Angels of translucent white, which move in and out at the top of the room where the subject is. They are tasked with determining the transition of the human body from human existence to ascension preparedness. They visit all humans that are nearing the period of ascension and determine the time to call in the next set of Angels. Humans register their ascension desires with these Angels.

Finishing Angels— These hard-working Angels are much smaller than others. They measure approximately twelve to fourteen inches in length. They are very wispy and white in appearance, and it is difficult to make out all their features unless closer examination is granted. Wispy, white clouds in the sky are representative of how these Angels look. They are entities of pure love and devotion. They move very quickly and then hover an inch or two above the resting human soul. A generous number of these Angels works simultaneously on one human soul and can remain with their assignment for as long as there is work required. This could be hours or days. They work independently; but because of the number in attendance, they sometimes appear to overlap or work on top of one another. It is their job to detach all cords that are not intended to travel with the soul. They also are tasked with embedding the cords of memories, lessons, and experiences that will remain with the soul to aid them with the development of their next life mission statement.

An additional duty has been given to these Angels as a result of the new shift to higher awareness and higher frequency communications. This new duty has lengthened the period of time that these Angels work on the assignment. They are now responsible for releasing all lower and negative energies that are still holding onto the soul. As they pluck lower/negative energy off, they whirl it closely to themselves at speeds that make it appear a blur. The transformation of the spun energy shifts its polarity from negative to positive and then to light dust and last to Divine light.

Timing Angels—As with the surveillance Angels, these Angels move quickly in and out to monitor progression. They are smaller than the Surveillance Angels and are more opaque. They have a responsibility for the exact timing of ascension. Per the request of the soul they are attending, they will give instructions that the ascension can begin. Many souls are very clear that they wish to wait until all loved ones are present prior to their ascension.

Alignment Angels— These Angels operate behind the scene and are rarely seen. They are semitransparent, white and light gray with a distinct feathery facade. Alignment Angels orchestrate the timing of the Angels in the correct progression.

They are instrumental in aligning all the souls to receive the newly ascended soul; this includes passed loved ones.

Escort Angels—These magnificently imperial Angels are significant in stature and are easily identifiable by their sizeable wings of brilliant shimmering white. These Angels lower themselves into the room and come to the side of a soul that is prepared to disengage from its human body and ascend. These Angels hold the soul in a loving manner to guide it on its ascension path. When these Angels lower themselves to the awaiting soul, they touch any other souls along their path. Humans who are within the radius of the ascending soul and are touched by these Angels often sense a shift and often experience a feeling of inner peace.

Life/Soul Review Angels—These patient Angels prepare a review of each soul's life lived. When a soul ascends it meets with an Angel from this department who provides a thorough review of its most recent life. The soul is allowed to look at its life without judgment to utilize the life as a tool to determine what the next life will be for the soul. These Angels are gracious and copious of medium to ample physique and their colors range from white to soft white with gray to light yellow intertwined.

Real-Life Angel Stories

T he following stories form the basis of the Angel encounters that are interwoven with the Angel teachings of *On An Angel's Wing*. The stories are reprinted here in the words of the contributors. I am very grateful for their generous sharing and humbled by each story of Angelic assistance.

Cross refer to real-life Angel story 1
Page 37

It was the middle of the night. Daniel was crying, so I picked him up and rocked him back to sleep. While I was rocking him to sleep, I fell asleep too. I felt someone tap me on the shoulder. When I woke up, no one was there. However, the arm that was holding Daniel had straightened out and Daniel was just about ready to fall to the ground!!!

Courtesy of Jacki Williams McCormack

Cross refer to real-life Angel story 2
Page 38

It was a clear morning, no rain in sight, as I began my daily commute to work. I saw the semi-truck as I merged onto Interstate 84; he was in the left lane right next to me as I merged. I even saw his right blinker go on and thought nothing of it. But then he moved over, coming into my lane forcing me to the wall, and then began dragging me. I was helpless. I remember thinking, "This is it." You are going to die today in a hideous accident. It all happened so fast and yet was in slow motion. Suddenly the truck and the wall released their grip sending me and my little Geo Prism spinning across the lanes of traffic. I saw the cars coming at me and knew we were going to crash. It was unavoidable. I was out of control just spinning and spinning. Then, whoosh. My morning coffee spewed up and out all over me when I hit the median and stopped, facing traffic the wrong way. Neat as a pin I slammed into the median and the car stopped. I couldn't believe it. I started shaking like a leaf as a nurse who was on her way to work and witnessed the accident ran across the traffic to see if I was hurt. I wasn't. She kept asking me if I hit my head. No. I wasn't physically hurt in the least bit. I remember feeling my Angel had protected me. I should have hit all the cars that were coming my way as I was spinning across the lanes of traffic. There was no other explanation. Even the police officer who arrived on the scene said he was surprised, given the skid marks, that I didn't roll the car.

I *felt* her with me that day. My baby sister who passed away in 1978 was with me, and I believe she protected me from crashing into the oncoming cars and kept me from rolling. It was my first thought once the shaking stopped. How did I manage to get through this with only a few dents and dings? My Angel. That's how.

Courtesy of Debbie

Cross refer to real-life Angel story 3
Page 94

Justin lost a very close friend to a car accident when he was a junior in high school. On the day of the funeral at Sacred Heart Church in Medford, he was sitting towards the front of the church. He saw/felt Thomas (the deceased) walk past him down the pew touching people as he walked by. At our house, he woke up one night and went out of his bedroom to find Thomas standing in the hallway. Justin was pretty shook up about Thomas' death. One night, while he was driving home from his girlfriend's house, Thomas appeared to him as he was driving and told him to live his life even though Thomas couldn't. Maybe that is not an angel story, but it truly touched him.

Courtesy of Justin Frantz via Mary Newdall-
Frantz

Cross refer to real-life Angel story 4
Page 106

As you know, my story has to do with the passing of our friend Sean; he took his own life last Feb. I had been having a hard time accepting this and wondered to myself if Sean would ever show me "a sign" that he was good and ok. What would it look like? A sighting? a weird noise? what? I decided that it would be a light bulb going out. Not any light bulb, a certain light bulb. The light fixture in our bathroom has 5 halogen bulbs, which never go out, they last forever. It would be one of these bulbs, it would be the bulb at the far right, above my wife's sink because she received a msg from Sean just prior to him taking his life. Within 2 or 3 days of me deciding this scenario, it happened! I was home alone, the kids at school, my wife at work. I walked into the bath, turned on the light. Poof! Out it went, the exact light bulb I decided would be the one. Was I crazy? Did this really happen? Did Sean show me "a sign" or was this merely a coincidence?? I hope this story is detailed enough. Good luck, Tim.

Courtesy of Tim McCormack

Cross refer to real-life Angel story 5
Page 175

. . .yes; and there's the one about when we were moving back from Cali and we were unloading the TWO rental trucks, up the driveway, up all the steps into the house, and it was raining (of course), and then we saved the refer for the very last thing to unload, and we started up the steps, and we got it stuck between the railings of the bottom set of steps, and it wouldn't budge, and we had nothing left to give, all three of us tugging on it and it wouldn't budge an inch, and I just closed my eyes and put my head on the refrigerator and said, "Oh please, God, we have nothing more to give, please help us get this into the house. "Before I even finished the sentence I heard someone right next to me—my eyes were still closed and he said, "Hi, it looks like you guys need some help." He said he lived across the street and had been watching us. This is the fastest prayer I have ever had answered!! Needless to say, he helped us get the refer unstuck and into the house in moments!!!

Courtesy of Margaret McIsaac-Kiyokawa

Cross refer to real-life Angel story 6
Page 181

Hello there. Hey, that's a pretty good story about the nail in the tire. It reminds me of a time once that Ross, Greg, a friend of Greg's and I were camping up at Green Peter Res. We were camping on the other side of the lake with boat access only. We had used up the gas in the boat so wanted to go to town and get more. We did this at night time, so not to cut into the daylight hours time for having fun. The plan was for Greg and his friend to stay at camp by the lake and have a big bonfire burning to mark our camp, while Ross hung out in the boat at the boat ramp where the pickup was parked and while I went into town to get more gas. I got the gas came back up to the boat ramp, and there was Ross waiting for me. We loaded the gas and headed to camp at the back of the reservoir. There was a low line of steam coming off the water so having the running lights on the boat blinded us to where we could not see. I ran wide open with lights off back up to where our camp was. But as we were continuing up the reservoir we could not see the "big fire" that Greg was supposed to have. Then on the shore we saw a lantern waiving back and forth. Oh, I thought, there is Greg. I stopped the boat and shut it off, to hear some guy say, "STOP, YOU ARE AT THE END OF THE RESERVOIR." I turned on a spotlight to find about 50 yards in front of us were stumps sticking out of the water. Then we looked back down the bank and here is another small light where Greg was.

I would say that guy was our angel that night! If we would of continued for less than 10 more seconds at full speed we would of hit these stumps and been catapulted out of the boat in the dark and who knows? Death is what I think would of happened. So that is one of my best stories.

Courtesy of Martin Mealue

Cross refer to real-life Angel story 7
Page 184

I almost got up right after this happened to write it down right away. I was having trouble sleeping last night and woke up around the 3:15 time frame. Tossed & turned, watched TV. Dozed in and out. I was laying on my stomach and in a dream state. dreaming about being in a car, but driving it on my stomach and operating it like an iPad. I finally decided to use the steering wheel to turn the car instead of using the palm of my hand. At one point, I got the car pointing in the right direction and was just laying there (on my car and in my bed). Suddenly there was a warm vibrating sensation at the base of my head, just to the right of where the spine enters the skull. I wondered what that was but it was nice, and then from that point, this warm, vibrating light moved slowly down my body filling me with warmth and, I think, light and lifting me up slowly into a standing position, but not firmly standing, more floating. It went completely through my body. When it started happening, I remember thinking that I was going to get to experience levitating. I think maybe I came into more of an awake state or maybe was thinking more than feeling, but then it went away and I was awake. Not an abrupt departure of the feeling, but just gone. I'm not sure how long it lasted, seconds at most I'm sure, but it did fill my body through to my feet. I honestly felt like I was being filled with a loving spirit. It felt so good and real and right. This was about 4:30 this morning.

Very cool.

Courtesy of Misty Tracy

Cross refer to real-life Angel story 8
Page 195

In 2004 around Thanksgiving, my son was in severe pain in his abdomen; he had been in pain for weeks and had never seen a doctor. We were all together on Thanksgiving and everyone asked him to go see a doctor; the very next day he did. I received a call at work from his wife, she told me that his appendix needed to come out and that he was being admitted into the hospital immediately. Everyone from both sides of the family were as at the hospital. I arrived in time to speak with my son, and I told him, "Everything will be just fine and don't worry." The doctor told us that the operation would take about 45 minutes. After about an hour and a half I had a very bad feeling; I knew something was wrong. I went to the Chapel and pleaded with God not to take him; he has 2 young children and his whole life ahead of him, I asked God to take me instead. That's when I felt a large warm hand on my left shoulder, and all I heard was, "He's strong," in a very deep voice. I got up off of my knees, and when I stood I could feel all of my worries lift up and out of my body. I still get goose bumps on my arms when I tell this part of the story. I left the Chapel and when I walked up to where everyone was waiting, the doctor came out and the first words out of his mouth were, "He's a very strong man." I almost hit the floor. I was shaking when I told everyone what had happened in the Chapel. Evidently my son's appendix had burst weeks before, but his fat tissue had surrounded the appendix and kept the gangrene from going into his system."

Courtesy of J. L.

Cross refer to real-life Angel story 9
Page 203

Cross refer to real-life Angel story 9
Page 203

Then, on my birthday this year, 12/12/12 (the Chinese say that 12/12/12 is the most spiritual day ever)

I was pouring my first cup of coffee and I could feel the warmth of 2 sets of arms hugging me. I didn't see them or hear anything, but somehow I knew it was my Mom and Dad holding me and wishing me a happy birthday! Mom and Dad are both in heaven.

I am so blessed. I know without a doubt that our loved ones are with us and they are our guardian angels!

Thanks for letting me tell my story, I love telling it. Courtesy of J.L.

Cross refer to real-life Angel story 10
Page 211

My Great Aunt helped raise me when I was born; my mom had many back surgeries & couldn't. I was a very quiet & shy child. I spent the 1st 6 years of my life with my aunt both at her house in the summer & when she stayed with my family. She was 57 when I was born; her husband had died the year before. They couldn't have kids so I was her "baby." She was wonderful, had unconditional love. She always said she could never leave & "go home," as she called it, until I was grown &

had someone to take care of me. She always had heart trouble.

My aunt had been a minister in the 1930's—1950's; she loved her bible. She kept a piece of my hair from when I was a baby in it, & and would write in **red** in it for specific sayings. As I grew up I got busy with life but would drive up to visit her when I could. She really lived for me. I loved her dearly. When I was 17 I got engaged; she met my fiancé. A few months later her heart started failing and she was in the hospital. I went every day to be with her, just talk, hold her hand.

She always told me to ask my angels for help when I was little. She made it a week, I was devastated, felt so alone, [it was] the 1st time I had dealt with death. That night my mom had me drive her to the store. I could do nothing but cry even in the store. Then in the store an old man walked up to me, handed me a tiny bible. He said, "Here this is for you to read now." I looked in my hand, looked up a second later, & he was gone, nowhere in the store. My mom had not seen him. We walked around trying to find him, he had vanished. I opened the bible & in **red writing,** it had some words. . .it was her exact handwriting, matched letters I had of hers! These were the same tiny bibles my aunt used to give us growing up!

"I told my very spiritually connected Nana when we got home; she said, "Honey, that was an angel from Aunt Annie! She is OK & with you still."

Courtesy of Stephanie A.

Cross refer to real-life Angel story 11
Page 218

When I was in my early thirties, I would spend hours after work and on weekends in the late fall making dried flower arrangements and wreaths to sell during the holidays at various bazaars. It used to supplement my single-mom income nicely and help provide a good Christmas for my beautiful son. Since the time period for making the arrangements and "getting them to market," so to speak, was a condensed time, I worked feverously to produce as much product as possible. One of these years was challenging because I lost my father in August. It was a very difficult loss for me, especially considering the events prior to his passing. I was not aware of the tools that I am now aware of for clearing and not carrying the pain. In early November, I got sick. Knowing that I needed to continue making product, I forced myself to work late into the nights and then would get up, get my son ready for school, and go to my job. I did not have time to get sick and I would just power through it. I finally had to break down and go to a doctor. He told me I had bronchitis and gave me a sulfa medication. A week later, I was worse, barely able to walk, my head bent to one side in pain, I could not straighten it out. I finally had to ask to be taken to urgent care. When I arrived at the urgent care, there was of course a waiting room full of people, each waiting to be seen by a doctor. Finally, my turn. I was shown to a room; then again, the wait. I was happy to be in the private room because I could lie down on the examining table and sleep. Sometime later the nurse came in and asked me to stand, which was challenging for me. She checked my blood pressure and a couple of other things, which I honestly do not remember now, and then exited the room. More waiting for me, more sleeping. The doctor entered the room next, followed by the nurse. Though most of this experience is still a blur to me, I was able to recognize their expressions of concern. The doctor did the same simple tests as the nurse had performed, double-checking her assessment I imagine. After completing his examination, the faces of concern worsened as they studied me. They told me they needed to call an ambulance to take me to the emergency room of the closest hospital. Since I had my friend drive me to the urgency care, I declined transportation via ambulance and accepted another ride to the emergency room, though I cannot really remember the ride.

The urgent care center had called ahead. Once there, I was examined from head to foot, given an IV, tested for spinal meningitis, tested for everything that they could think of. I was admitted into the hospital. By day three, I was not getting any better and there were still no answers. This hospital transferred me via ambulance to a larger hospital, with specialists to examine me.

I remember one day lying in the hospital bed, and a doctor brought in a group of interns. They were using me as a case study; I remember the doctor saying, "We do not know what is wrong with her," and then listed several medical terms that I did not understand. There was a conversation about me, heads shaking back and forth, brows bunched in a sign of confusion. I just wanted to sleep. I lost track of time.

Then something happened. As I lay in bed sleeping, something woke me up. I looked around and no one was there. I turned my gaze to the ceiling, beyond the ceiling really, to heaven. I began talking to God. You see, I was scared. My grandfather had died in this very hospital. This hospital was also the last one that my mother was a patient in before she was sent home to die. I was sick with what was still undetermined and I was not getting better, but rather slipping everyday despite the varied treatments. I told God and the Angels that I was not ready to die, that I was afraid. I could feel tears forming in my eyes.

The next thing that happened still covers me with truth bumps when I think about it. The door to the bathroom, which was positioned to my left, began opening slowly without assistance from anyone. I was then enveloped in a scent I could not identify; it seemed like a medicinal smell overlaid with flowers. I was completely taken aback and again examined the room for a sign of a nurse or someone who could have triggered the door moving, the scent shrouding me. Then a blanket of calm covered me, I was filled with knowingness that I had been saved, I had been sent Angels to heal me.

I immediately began getting better. The doctors were baffled. They still had not determined my illness; but out of necessity, I believe, diagnosed me with three different conditions. Two days later I went home.

Though the doctors were not able to establish with certainty what had ailed me, I know what was wrong with me. I had suffered a broken heart. I felt abandoned and unloved by my father; and, instead of voicing those things to him when he was alive, I kept them inside of me to fester. It is imperative that you learn to forgive and release all negatives. Carrying them around every day, bringing them up at will to rehash and toil over does no good. It does in fact do harm. It creates more negative energy for you, for those you are around, and for the world. Remember the lesson and let go of the negative emotion.

Author, Marilyn Lawrence

Cross refer to real-life Angel story 12
Page 223

A couple of years after my mother's breast cancer, my mother was calling in sick to work. She was just having a hard time getting out of bed. Her awful, mean, good-for- nothing boss insisted she get a doctor's note before she was allowed to come back to work. What a horrible, nitpicky boss, right??? Had my mother not have been required to go to the doctor to get a note, she may not have discovered that her lungs were hardening and she was dying!!!! And of course you know the rest of the story!!!"

Thank you, Angels, for that horrible boss.

Courtesy of Jacki Williams-McCormack

Cross refer to real-life Angel story 13a and 13b
Page 241

When I was approximately thirteen years old, I went on a trip with my parents and my sister, Margaret. Though I have always told my niece, Janie, my sister's daughter, that her mother is older than me by four years, I must, for clarification in this story, admit that I am in fact four years older than my sister. My sister, therefore, was approximately nine years old. We were visiting the World's Fair and staying in a hotel that was joined to another hotel by a rooftop swimming pool. It was the first day at the fair and our father took us swimming in the late afternoon to cool off from the hot day at the fair. There were, at that time, a group of six adults enjoying themselves by the pool with libations and laughs. The three of us enjoyed a swim while my mother, I am sure, happy to have some time to herself, stayed in the room. We finished our swim, gathered our things, and then headed down the stairs to our room. After dinner my sister asked to go swimming again, as the pool did not close until 10:00 pm. My sister was always resolute in her pursuit of something she wanted; and actually not much has changed in that regard, much to her credit. She stayed after the idea until my father eventually caved and took us both up the long flight of stairs to again enjoy a swim.

As we neared the top of the stairs we could hear voices coming from the pool area. When we turned the corner we could see that the same adults from our afternoon swim were still there. By this time, they had consumed alcohol for several hours and their actions represented that fact. My father initially wanted to leave so that we would not be subject to their behavior; but again my sister pleaded to stay and swim. We walked to the pool, my sister already removing her towel and sandals, ready to jump in.

At the corner of the deep end of the pool my father and I saw a male figure floating at the bottom of the pool. My father questioned the adults, who were laughing amongst themselves, about the gentleman, how long he had been in the pool, etc. The adults stopped just long enough to tell my father that their friend was playing a trick on them and pretending that he was drowning, but in reality he was just holding his breath.

My father begged to differ with them. He bent over and looked more closely at the gentleman on the bottom of the pool and then without hesitation told me to jump in and pull the man to the top of the water so he could pull him out of the pool. The gentleman's friends were cackling and continued to maintain their stance that their friend was pretending.

The lifeless body floated to the surface of the water under my direction. My father then instructed me to get out and help pull the body out of the water. The gentleman's friends were still laughing and correcting my father's actions, though in a softer tone the more they observed.

When the gentleman was securely out of the water, my father rolled him on his stomach and had me place my hands below his face at which point my father preceded to perform resuscitation until the man spit and coughed out water struggling to breathe. Dazed as to why he was in the position he was in, the man began swinging his fists at whatever was close and, of course, that was my father and me. My sister saw this and began screaming. By this time the man's friends had gathered around realizing that it was no longer a game of holding breath.

If my sister had not been so insistent that we go swimming again (kudos to my sister!), if my father had not known how to give artificial resuscitation, and if I had not been there to lend a hand, that gentleman more than likely would not have seen the following day.

Sometimes Angels give us messages that are very important. They make us have a burning desire to go swimming a second time, even though we really do not want to. They give us strength beyond what is normal; they guide us to a special location. We need always to pay attention to these things. If you have a burning desire to do something or go somewhere that does not make sense to you at the time, but you just know you need to do it, then you need to do it. The message is coming for you.

I have often thought about that gentleman and wondered if he ever knew that if it were not for the Angels giving my sister the message to go swimming, then who knows how his *then* would be.

I shared the above story with my sister before printing this book. The following are her comments on the event.

Author, Marilyn Lawrence

13b

I do remember that swimming story, too. . .although not the exact details like you because I am so much younger. I remember that we went up earlier to swim and the adults there were partying so much and being so rowdy with such foul language that Mom said that we could not stay and that we could come back later. Of course I did not let anyone forget that! So back we went, and that is when you and Dad found the guy underwater and hopped in to get him and then the guy came to and started swinging and running after everyone. I was terrified. Dad said, "I need to get these girls out of here," and with that I was off running without looking back, thinking the crazy guy was after me!!! I know that I almost gave Mom a heart attack when I hit the motel door, which swung open when I hit it!!!

Courtesy of Margaret McIsaac-Kiyokawa

Cross refer to real-life Angel story 14a and 14b
Page 248

When David was first admitted into the hospital for having a stroke, the doctor came into the room to check on him. He was having bleeding in his brain and they were undecided whether they needed to send him off to a more advanced hospital than we have in Newport. The doctor asked a few questions of David and asked him to move his limbs, and to walk around if he could. He did as he was asked, and then the doctor asked him some questions, and got a very puzzled look on her face, and said she needed to check on something. She left the room and I was very confused why she left so suddenly and why she didn't tell us anything, as it seemed like hours I had been waiting to hear what was going on, hours and hours (it seemed like), worrying and worrying. The Doctor did come back into the room and she apologized for leaving so suddenly earlier. She said that she had looked at David's test results before she had come into the room the first time and had expected to see someone that could not move their the whole right side of their body and who could not speak. She said she couldn't believe that she was watching him walk around without difficulty and carry on a conversation, and she had to go out and look at the test results again to make sure she had the right person. She said that we were very lucky, that with the extreme damage in two areas of the brain, David should be paralyzed. I told her luck had nothing to do with it!

The next day, when we were waiting for more tests to determine whether he would have to have any surgery to stop the bleeding in the brain or he would have to be transferred to another hospital, brought another miracle. The tests came back completely clean. No bleeding- none- it was completely gone!! Amen!

Courtesy of Margaret McIsaac-Kiyokawa

14b

My sister Margaret called me on her drive to the hospital; her voice came through strained and frazzled. I immediately knew it was not a social call. She proceeded to tell me that her husband, David, had just had a stroke and she was racing to the hospital from work. Margaret was beside herself because she lived a few hours from any family and at that moment she felt completely alone. She told me that she had called both John, our brother, and me. When neither of us answered, she struggled with the idea of being all alone and handling such a huge occurrence by herself. She just did not know what to do, who to call, how she could handle this; and so she began to pray during the forty-five-minute drive to the hospital, which felt like eternity, asking God and the Angels to help her and to help David.

I got home and packed my bag, not knowing how long I would be gone and what to expect. When I arrived in the town of Newport, I went straight to the hospital to check on David. My brother had just arrived and we were met by Margaret and the miraculous news of David's ability to be so mobile considering the magnitude of his stroke damage. Since there were still tests to be run and a lot of "could-be's and might-be's," the tension was still running high. I planned on staying with my sister until I was no longer needed. As the days passed, miraculous news about David's condition continued to Grace us. The outpouring of good wishes and noble deeds that Margaret, David, and Janie received from their friends, co-workers, and church members was humbling and passionate. It was very evident that my sister and her family were not alone and would never be alone in any sense.

One night, which proved to be my last night at my sister's home, I had a dream. It was a beautiful dream in that my mother (who passed twenty-some years earlier) visited me. We were at my maternal grandparents' home, which was a beautiful old four-story home filled with stained glass, incredible furniture, happy memories, and stellar hiding places. I can remember loving going to my grandparent's home as a child, especially when my cousins were there; the laughter, happy memories, and games of hide-and seek were unsurpassed! As dreams sometimes go, travels, experiences, and ideas flash in and out, not following a clear pattern. Such was the case with this dream.

As I played in the rooms with my cousins, I looked out one of the bedroom windows and, much to my surprise, several owls were perched in a large tree looking back at me. My mother walked in the room, and at that point I realized that my Aunt Louise was sitting on the bed. My mother asked Aunt Louise if she would like to accompany her to some classes. My aunt respectfully declined and told my mother that she wanted to go shopping with Gracie's children instead.

I woke up early the next morning clearly recalling my dream. The dream brought to light two different things, but it was a while before I realized the second. The first realization was that I did not have to worry about David any longer because my mother did not even mention him in the dream; the only other person in the dream was my aunt. This message came loud and clear to me. I utilized my dream as my sign from my loved ones in Heaven that all was fine with David.

What I did not realize until much later was that, at the same time that David was suffering from his incident, Aunt Louise herself was terribly ill and had been found in her home alone barely alive. This is another example of the importance of paying attention to the messages that you receive.

Aunt Louise has recovered and has moved closer to family. David does still have effects of the stroke but is working very hard each day to gain back complete health. It is a Divine miracle that the effects that he faces daily are tremendously less than what the x-rays and tests told the doctor he should be suffering. Both David and my aunt are surrounded by the love of family and friends and, of course, God and his Angels!

Author, Marilyn Lawrence

Cross refer to real-life Angel story 15
Page 272

You know I have a lot of stories I could talk about, but one of my favorites is below.

Back in the 70's when I was a college kid, always jetting off to Europe to backpack on my own, I had a serious Angel intervention: I had just spent a crazy, amazing month in Istanbul and had to leave. My good friend from NYC was maybe going to meet me in Paris in few days and I needed to be there just in case. Ability to communicate was limited back then—no cell phones and wi-fi. It was fine; the plan was to consider being there if she showed and ok if not, plenty to do in Paris and beyond, or not.

I was planning to fly the once-a-day Air France from Athens this time, because I had left Turkey late and I still needed to be at University in Stockholm in less than a month.

Long train ride to Athens. I was lucky. I was on time to catch the flight stand by. My parents were nervous about me being in Turkey and were relieved it was time for me to get to Paris and be closer to my destination of school. I switched trains in Athens to head to the airport. I was almost at the airport when, for no reason at all, I was in a hurry to get off the train and go back to Athens and not go. I fought it. It was stronger and stronger to get off the train, do not pass go, do not go to PARIS. I got off the train, bewildered, and went back to Athens hoping my friend didn't go to PARIS

after all (turned out she didn't). I am feeling guilty but
stood my ground and refused for no reason to follow
thru. I decided to be selfish and just jump a boat and
head to an island in the Aegean Sea instead. I was
bewildered over my decision-making process; this was
not my norm. So I went off to the island and had a great
time.

The Air France Flight I was scheduled to be on
from Athens to Paris was HIJACKED. It was a terrorist
highjack as the flight was full of Israeli tourists. You
may recall the famous flight to UGANDA and the sick
dictator IDI AMIN who loved to feed people to the
crocodiles. I, of course, look Israeli with my wild hair
and skin color etc., clear Middle East background. Many
were shot just on an assumption of what they were. This
was a huge international event with Israeli war jets
risking war with LIBYA and flying over Gaddafi's
airspace to rescue who they could; it almost brought on
a full-on war in the Middle East. My parents were
beyond terrified, no word from me, and I was supposed
to be on that plane. That was when my Mom went grey
from pure gorgeous black hair. My family's community
was in devastation waiting. I had no idea what-so-ever. I
carried on in Greece, then trained to Stockholm barely
on time to start the semester. I called home only because
I needed some extra money. I had chipped my tooth in

Rome on huge bottle of wine and needed to get to a dentist. My parents were sobbing.

Then I found out what happened; I was shocked. My mother asked me how was it I didn't get on that plane as was the plan. I told her, "I don't know why; I was almost to the airport and my brain kept telling me don't go, no, no, skip this event." I had decided to go with my gut this time is all. THANK GOD.

A couple of years later in my International Law class back at MSU, I wrote a brief about the hijacking that wound up at the Pentagon and is on file regarding that international airspace violation. The brief was used for military decisions and airspace violations. The U.S. was in a position that, should war break out, they would have to defend Israel despite the Israelis having violated Libya because they didn't care about law; they had been attacked and citizens had died.

Small world, a friend was in London when this happened and recalled the family was on hold in Heathrow while such a dangerous world event, hijack of a jetliner, occurred.

I, to this day, will swear it was a higher power intervention; there was NO reason for me not to make that flight, none. I have never, ever stood anyone up and I acted in that capacity by not getting on that flight. The higher power decided it wasn't my time.

Thanks for listening.

Courtesy of Susan Baha-Vogel

Cross refer to real-life Angel story 16
Page 272

About ten months after my ex-husband told me
that he no longer wanted to be married and we were in
the finalization of our divorce, I experienced a moment
that I will never forget. It was getting dark and I was in
my backyard watering my grass, thinking about how in
the world was I going to be able to raise my two
daughters on my own, stay in my house, and work full
time. I had whispered and asked God to show me a sign
that I am going to be fine and that everything would
work out. At that moment as I was watering I saw a
glitter of gold sparkle through the air. At first I thought
it was the reflection of the water and the street light, but
it was larger than the spray of water and it floated for
what seemed to be like three to four seconds. I wanted
to run into the house and tell my daughters, but I
thought they would think I was crazy. Then I didn't
want to tell anyone because I thought if I did I would
struggle in life. The rest of the evening I couldn't stop
thinking about what I had just experienced and

suddenly felt at peace. I then knew I was going to be okay and so would my daughters. This happened 13 years ago and only about two years ago I told my experience. To this day I have raised two beautiful daughters; I'm still in my house; and have a good job. I'm blessed and very lucky. Still single though, but that's okay. :)

Courtesy of Bridgitt Calder

Cross refer to real-life Angel story 17
Page 279

My mom died in 1988. In 2004 I was going through a **long harassing,** stressful divorce fighting for my 2 sons. At work one day I had been worn down from it all; my health was not good. I locked up the business doors, sat on the floor in back & broke down & cried & cried, depleted & worn down.

I kept my great aunt's bible she had from the 1930's; I would hug it when really down. I had it at my business since our house was for sale & so many people were going through it. I wanted it at my business since I spent 10 hours a day there. I picked up the bible off the shelf & there underneath was a little paper. It said, "I said a prayer for you today. I asked god that he be near you at the start of each day, grant you health & blessings. I asked for happiness for you, all things big & small, but for his loving care most of all." At the bottom **signed in red was** "My love, mom" in my mom's handwriting this time. I was stunned, asked my sons if they had seen that; they hadn't. My oldest said, "Mom, you know who left that" (the three above—my mom, my great aunt & my Nana). Wise son. I felt like I got a big hug & knew we were being watched over & all would be OK.

    I am grateful for the experiences I have had. My mom, Nana & aunt were all VERY physic. My aunt was the minister who was connected; my Nana was the wild one for her day. She did astral flight, was very much into the spiritual world, past lives. She & I used to go to Ananda in LA in the 70's. She was very connected, the "new age" manifesting. She had friends who would do psychometry; she taught me the power of words! I grew up knowing all this but then got married to non-believers, so I kind of got away. It feels better to be back to what I know after my divorce. My sons got it; at their young age they are very old souls! I was lucky also going through my divorce to have had a lady that channeled an ascended master to guide me & my sons.

There was a weird text I got on my mom's birthday, when I had been concerned about my son. I didn't know the Ph#. When I Googled, the name was her maiden name in Sparks but a man's first name, instead of Donna, it was Don!

My great aunt always had coffee by her bedside at night. I would always smell it as I snuggled up to sleep with her when I was about 4; the smell of coffee instantly makes me think of her. Again when I was at my most stressed a few years ago, I woke up about 3 am smelling STRONG COFFEE. I got up, went downstairs to see if my son was up making coffee, but he was sound asleep. Then I got it & said, "Thanks Aunt Annie." I knew she was with me.

Same thing in the 90's. My 2 sons & I went down to my sister's house. She wanted to put flowers on my mom's grave; we had not been there since she died 9 years earlier. My dad remarried & his wife didn't want us in his life, so he stopped talking to us. I knew my mom was not there, but we did it. That night we were in my sister's living room when we got the strong smell of gardenias. It was my mom's favorite cologne & she had them planted outside of her house. My sister was a bit freaked out. I just said mom is here and she's letting & us know. These things always happen when I am feeling alone, not sure what to do; it reminds me all is always well & to shift into a good feeling. I am blessed to have the love that never goes away. "

Courtesy of Stephanie A.

Cross refer to real-life Angel story 18
Page 284

I also had another experience that I believe saved mine and my brother's life. We were young. We were both riding on the same bicycle. Remember those bikes with the banana seats? It was one of those. We were riding through a campground when I had a déjà vu advance on me. You know that when you are experiencing déjà vu, it's in the moment? Well this one advanced on me and I saw the future. I saw us entering an intersection and a Winnebago camper hit us!!! So I screamed to my brother to stop and I jumped off the bike just before we entered the intersection. And just as I jumped off, guess what drove by?????

Yup....a Winnebago!

Courtesy of Jacki Williams McCormack

Cross refer to real-life Angel story 19
Page 291

When Michelle first learned to drive, she was able to drive to school on her own-about 5 miles away on country roads. One day, right after she left for an evening "air band" practice, she called to say that she had rolled her car about 1 mile from the house. She assured me that she was okay. Justin and I flew out of the house and arrived at the scene: her car was still on its roof with the tires rolling, in a field. She had left the road and over corrected while reaching for something and careened off the road, through a wire field fence and just missing a power pole. She was traveling about 50 miles an hour-the speed limit for that part of the road.

She explained that when she crawled out of the car and crawled through the fence to the road, there was an elderly lady that stood next to her, keeping her company. She said that she didn't know where she went—she just disappeared. Michelle was completely unharmed physically in the accident but was highly emotional when she saw her car the next day where we had parked it next to the barn.

Courtesy of Michelle Frantz via Mary Newdall-Frantz

Cross refer to real-life Angel story 20
Page 298

My husband, Dale, was home for the weekend, and I had to drive him to the airport at very early dark-thirty in the morning to fly to a job. As we started the drive, I heard a noise coming from what I thought was a tire. I asked Dale to listen; but as some of us know, too many years of loud rock and roll have left Dale with less than perfect hearing, hence he could not hear the sound. At the point the sound became very loud, he was able to hear it. Driving along, I isolated the sound as coming from the back passenger side tire. Dale got out, looked at the tire, and checked for a flat or something in the tire. He found nothing and we continued to the airport so that he would not miss his flight. I had a very bad feeling though, and all the way to the airport and back home I asked the Angels to surround the car with love and to keep us safe. I called the Bluelight in for our drive as well.

My son, Michael looked at the tire when the sky lightened and found a nail. He took the car to the tire shop for me when it opened. Come to find out three lug nuts were sheared off and had fallen in the rotor and a fourth had fallen off completely. The tire consultant said the wheel could have fallen off the car at any second. It took getting a nail in the tire for us to know this had happened. A nail not in any tire, but in the tire that was ready to fall off! There are no accidents, unless you forget to pay attention to the messages sent to you.

Thank you, Angels, for everything you do for us every day and for sending us a nail that very well could have saved our lives! I am humbled and appreciative!

Author, Marilyn Lawrence

Cross refer to real-life Angel story 21
Page 300

About my angel story, the main one that I can think about is the day that Eli was born. There had been a HORRIBLE winter storm, 84 was closed, everything was iced over, and I went into labor. When Elizabeth was born at 11:15 a.m. on the 10th, the sun came out and all of the cold and winter started melting away and in my arms I held the most amazing miracle that would change my life from that day on. That's the best one I can think about. I hope you like it!"

Courtesy of the author's beautiful niece

Megan McIsaac-Ruiz

Cross refer to real-life Angel story 22
Page 305

Years ago my father-in-law, Larry, passed away. Just after his passing, I had gone into Subway to pick up some lunch and take it back to work. As I got my lunch I started walking out of Subway and noticed an older man sitting in a booth by himself. I didn't think anything of it until I walked by him. As I was going by his table, he looked up at me a smiled at me. I smiled back at him and kept walking. As I was looking at him, I stared right into his eyes and felt like I was looking in the eyes of Larry. I immediately got a chill and wanted to go back and look at him again, but felt strange doing that, so I didn't. I kept walking and then I smiled and thought to myself that Larry was with me for a moment and wanted me to know that he was doing just fine and out of pain. I couldn't wait to get home and tell my daughters. When I told them they had chills themselves because they told me that they just had a recent dream of him and he was very happy. We were all very close and at the end of his death he was in a lot of pain. I truly believe he entered our lives to let us know that he is okay.

Courtesy of Bridgitt Calder

Cross refer to real-life Angel story 23
Page 311

Ok. I know you remember this story but will refresh you a bit. We were living in the big white house. At different times, Sandy would tell me she heard someone walking around upstairs, but I had never heard anything.

One night when I was sleeping, I woke to this feeling someone was there. I was facing the hallway sleeping on my side. As I opened my eyes, I saw this whitish cloud right in front of me. I froze and stared; then suddenly it was gone. I woke Sandy and told her about it, but she really didn't believe me.

Finally after mom died, I had that same feeling again: someone was there. I opened my eyes and out in the hallway was this beautiful bluish-colored ball floating and rotating. I woke Sandy and she saw it too. It was mom checking on us and telling me there is a God and a beautiful Heaven. She floated there for some time then left.

There you go. Hugs. Love you.

      Courtesy of author's beloved brother, John
McIsaac

An Earth Angel Tribute

I was moved to tears when I received the following story. This comes from a gentleman who attended one of my husband's classes. Little did I know that one of the first Angel stories I would receive would be about my husband!

A special thank you goes out to Jonathan, for these beautiful words of tribute!

Send Me an Angel
(The Naughty Boy Has Cleared the Way)

There it was 2002; Grey Davis Governor of California had destroyed many businesses by raising Workers Comp rates and taxes. The evil government worker (Bureaucrat cum laude) was recalled and got his

Page 385

comeuppance after leaving the remnants of a Roman battlefield; bodies bleeding out and vultures descending to pick the cold carrion. My personnel service which I had started from the kitchen table, had been crushed by Big Brother. Herculean efforts availed naught. (Send me an Angel.)

I had employed hundreds of people and had gotten billing up to a couple of million, but now not only were my employees out of work but so was I. What to do? I knew I had to retrain myself in a legitimate profession, but how and where? Milled around for a year or two contemplating the issue. (Send me an Angel.)

Got an insurance license but could not sell a policy…wasn't for me. At the same training location, I heard the real estate class instructor next door talking in the distance (Small Angel, perhaps a pre-whisper from the main event; see below) and took the plunge, studied for the exam. Took the exam but knew that the government license was just what "they" wanted you to know and would not ensure success in the field, as much of the information disseminated was of no practical consequence. (Send me an Angel.)

I interviewed with 18 real estate companies. Most were trash-sounding, out-pie-in-the sky policies and political correctness. No methodology, no true education; you would be thrown out into the fray without plan or protection, a sure path to failure. (Send me an Angel.)

This is when the clarion call and the floating down from on high occurred. I do not know whether it was Michael, Gabriel, Uriel, or Raphael but the flapping of the wings and the breeze it created summoned me. The darkness of ignorance was lifted and the correct path was laid out before me with a manly handshake and a welcoming visage.

This man, angel with a devil-may-care attitude, had been hired by a large California company to train people in real estate, and his name was inspiration and fun. His middle name was humanity for he was born with so much of it. His background was like all creative people of merit: varied, inventive, and adventurous.

It was decreed that this would be his last series of classes teaching with this company because the wealthy owner went with a robotic xxx-kiss teacher and treated this Angel with disrespect. Real Angels will not be treated with disrespect as they know their value.

Days of learning and opening the doors are how the angel communicated and sent his angelic message to those who had ears. An Angel can choose any vehicle from music to Sanskrit. They know not time and have mastered earthly forms. I mean after all, what is far to an Angel, to fly to a star or live a thousand million years? Eternally grateful for this foundation is how I will always feel. Stories and examples, methods and tasks can be recalled from training years ago to make a living even in bad markets. Eyes that see opportunity is what the angel laid upon my brow, me like verse from out his mouth. Solid learning and a lifetime of skills that can never die were imparted by the wafting of the wings and the opening of the gates. (Sent me an Angel…and I received it.)

I shall sing his praises until the day I meet the master. BTW One of the newly trained class of agents wrote a poem about him back then in 2004. See attached. I'm a Broker now with a few of my own agents and I went high and far, but to me the man I give the credit to is my teacher, Dale Lawrence.

God Bless Dale and Marilyn Lawrence. I love you both.

From freedoms gate we ring the bell
From up and down from high and hell
The cloudy mist is gone today
The naughty boy has cleared the way
Jonathan Taylor
9/30/2012

To Dale Lawrence (a cut above) by Jonathan Taylor

Gifted

From freedoms gate we ring the bell
From up and down from high and
hell
The cloudy mist is gone today
The naughty boy has cleared the
way
He showed us wisdom but more
than that
Before the meat hit the floor he'd
cut the fat
Up and down from high and hell
From freedoms gate we ring the bell
He laid upon a carpet red
All good things that he had said
And listening with attentive ear
We found a pathway through the
fear
The options appeared before our
beds
Strategically placed by teacher's
head
Teacher, teach, you gave us drink
So many weeks such time to think

To plan, to do, to walk, to phone
The drink you gave has made a
home
Hail, hail the naughty boy
He closed the sale he brought the
joy
Boldness is born where once was
dread
And be assured we're in good stead
For when the oppositions come
Your dialogue will be the chum
And when the bait is bitten through
We'll stand alone and stand with
you
Can you see the happy plan
For every woman and every man
Who dared to step into the house of
pain
Where every dose was all our gain?
Out into the world we'll go
Far away and never slow
And memories of you, what will
that be?
A mystic place of mystery?
Or will we recall the mystic chant
The chunking and what you did
plant

For here you taught and planted
trees
Of that there is no mystery
I like money but more than this
I like the way you treated us
Every time we interact
We'll know who gave us our strong
back
And every time that bell does ring
We'll hear your voice it sounds like
spring
From freedoms gate we ring the bell
From up and down from high and
hell
The cloudy mist is gone today
The naughty boy has cleared the
way
And where are we now?
Where were we led?
That place that keeps us in good
stead
What does it mean?
Where did we go?
Are you with me? Yes or no?
It means we have a place to stand
Firmly rooted in your plan

Waves may crash and winds may
blow

We'll fill the cup from where ere the
flow

A flipping funnel we'll put it in

And when we turn 'round you'll
see our grin

So when you're old and people are
rude

Think back upon our gratitude

If people don't appreciate

What you have done at this late
date

Then when you're sleeping soft and
sound

And all our spirits have gathered round

We'll lay some treasure at your feet

And then we'll all just take our seat

You'll suddenly hear our mystic chant

The ones who could from the ones who can't

And then you'll know deep in your heart

That you're the one who gave the start

You'll close the book on a life well spent

And wonder where the years all went

Page 393

Hail, Hail the naughty boy

He closed the sale he brought the

joy

Yes, we'll all be there when you're

old and grey

So remember, remember, remember

this day

From freedoms gate we ring the bell

From up and down from high and

hell

The cloudy mist is gone today

The naughty boy has cleared the

way.

Courtesy of Jonathan Taylor

Human or Angel or Master, we all have our own

Divine path to walk and key role to play.

Honor it, Honor others, Honor all!

Let us begin Now being the best we are to be!

About the Author

Throughout her, Marilyn Lawrence knew that there was a special purpose for her, but being a single mom and focusing on a busy career, she lost sight of her path. Then a series of unavoidable, undeniable experiences gave her the message loud and clear and made it difficult to avoid her purpose any longer.

An author and teacher, Lawrence's work is grounded in the strong belief that every person has been placed in this world with a special "Divine gift" to share and a purpose to guide them. With her passionate commitment to spiritual service through classes, retreats, personal readings and healings, she has helped many people remove obstacles in their lives so they can once again feel the infinite joy of their own purpose.

If you have stories of Angelic encounters that you would like shared in Marilyn's next book, please email them to marilyn@marilynlawrence.
Visit www.marilynlawrence.com for more information about Marilyn's books, classes and workshops.

Made in the USA
San Bernardino, CA
13 July 2018